Educate the Heart

Praise for *Educate the Heart: Screen-Free Activities for Grades PreK-6 to Inspire Authentic Learning*

"Don't be fooled by the title of *Educate the Heart*. This is not a book that is based solely on emotion. Quattrucci does a fantastic job of sharing practical and easy to understand methods for teaching children how to be successful in both school and in life. For teachers who care about their students beyond their abilities to just produce test scores."—Doug Campbell, author of *Discipline Without Anger and Essential Tips for Classroom Success*

"Sure, technology has its place in the classroom. But with her fun and engaging, yet no-nonsense style, Jennifer Lee Quattrucci has provided elementary school teachers a treasure-trove of practical actionable activities that lure kids away from the soul-sucking, zombie-flying effects of being glued to their screens 24/7 and into more mindful, present learning. You will not only find yourself learning so much from this book, you will enjoy it as well!"—Dan Tricarico, author of *The Zen Teacher: Creating Focus, Simplicity, and Tranquility in the Classroom*, @thezenteacher

"*Educate the Heart* by Jennifer Lee Quattrucci is a wonderful resource for teachers. We live in a world saturated with screens, and she provides excellent ideas for breaking away from technology and learning in more wholesome and engaging ways. I especially love her ideas for fostering kindness and community and for using literature in all aspects of learning. This is a must have for teachers!"—Stefanie Hohl, creator of *ABC, See, Hear, Do*

"Few educators are as imaginative, compassionate, and dedicated to student growth and well-being as the brilliant Jennifer Lee Quattrucci. This remarkable book unleashes students' imaginations and uniquely combines many innovative educational practices in helping students and teachers."—Scott T. Allison, professor of psychology and IRB chair, and editor of *Heroism Science*, @HeroesToday

"Teachers rarely get the credit they deserve for shaping the hearts and minds of the young people that come through their classrooms. The countless hours they put into crafting lesson plans that balance curriculum with innovative, thought provoking and attention capturing content often goes unnoticed, let alone appreciated. Today's educators have to compete with attention challenged students who have grown up with devices in their hands and are capable of absorbing information at a lightning pace. This means more and more pressure is put on teachers to keep learning both relevant and engaging at a level that aligns with how students experience things in today's real world.

"Jennifer Lee Quattrucci is a teacher that gets it. She understands the odds are stacked against her and yet year after year finds a way to make memorable connections with her students. She has managed to turn classroom success into the standard of helping students eclipse into higher levels of learning excellence. Jennifer's innovative approach to developing critical learning skills for her kids while delivering the mandated requirements dictated to by the formalized criteria shows just how impactful creative teaching strategies must be if success is to be found in today's classroom.

"I am personally inspired by the approach Jennifer Lee Quattrucci has demonstrated in her classroom and could not be more excited that she is willing to open her secrets to classroom success up to teachers everywhere. This powerful book will no doubt make a huge impact on new teachers and those who have taught for years. This book will no doubt change the way teachers think about reinventing a child's learning experience and developing a heartfelt approach to ensuring every student learns to love the process of learning. This book will no doubt create a Ripple Effect that can and will change the lives of the young people you are blessed to teach."—Steve Harper, entrepreneur, speaker, and author of The Ripple Effect: Maximizing the Power of Relationships for Your Life and Business, @Rippleon

"There is no shortage of theories, philosophies, activities, or mindsets for teaching written by non-classroom educators. In the era of education-reform, the notion of teachers and done unto them, rather than innovating collaboratively has been the norm. Jennifer Lee Quattrucci gives a platform and a guide for educators to reclaim the spark of discovery through inspiring anecdotes, experienced advice, and practical activities to engage, enlighten, and inspire elementary age children in a delightful and stylish way."—Alex Lucini, educator, activist, Providence School Department

"*Educate the Heart* is not only amazing, but it is a must have for all elementary school teachers! It's the students that will win when educators use this book to its fullest. Not only are there amazing and easy to implement lessons, but fantastic resources, quotes, and how-tos for every experience level of a teacher. Quattrucci uses her own experiences, failures, successes, and brilliance for this amazing work of HEART!" —Jeff Kubiak, elementary school principal, speaker, and author of *One Drop of Kindness*, @jeffreykubiak

"The relationships we build with our students set the foundation for our impact. Jennifer Lee Quattrucci does a wonderful job of providing a resource that offers step-by-step strategies that connect empathy, kindness, and community building with the power of learning. This book is jam packed with practical ideas that can be used in the classroom right away."—Chuck Poole, teacher, founder of Teachonomy, and producer of the uNseries, @cpoole27

"In her book, Educate the Heart, Jennifer Quattrucci provides the reader with a treasure trove of resources and lesson ideas that are woven together with the themes of Kindness,

Integration, and Fun! The ideas she presents come from over 20 years of classroom experience and move beyond teaching lessons to creating experiences for students. This is the book I wish I had when I was still in the classroom as a teacher. When asked the question, 'Would you want to be a student in your own classroom?' The answer would be a resounding yes, for anyone who implements the rich and vibrant ideas presented in this book. It will be on my recommendation list for all teachers, new and experienced!"—Jonathon Wennstrom, elementary principal, Livonia Public Schools, Michigan, @jon_wennstrom

"Jennifer Lee Quattrucci's *Educate the Heart: Screen-Free Activities for Grades PreK-6 to Inspire Authentic Learning* is full of over 150 practical, creative, and just plain brilliant ideas that address all components of social emotional learning while emphasizing the importance of critical thinking skills, important academic topics, and the power of effective collaboration.

"I am amazed at the way Jennifer has been able to put her 20-plus years of educating young children into such an informative, enjoyable resource that absolutely any educators, regardless of grade, subject, or level of expertise they may have, will benefit from and be able to use immediately. The ideas and all the content in this book magically join the great need for educating the heart with the goal of preparing students for future success in school, and more importantly, in life.

"Topics such as flexile seating, homework, STEM challenges, mathematical discourse, collaborative art, literacy centers, author studies, classroom management, and even cooking in the classroom are presented with clear goals, expectations, practical good sense, and a whole lot of developmentally appropriate fun!"—Nathan Maynard, Dean of Culture at Purdue Polytechnic High School; author of *Hacking School Discipline: 9 Ways to Create a Culture of Empathy & Responsibility Using Restorative Justice*; cofounder of Behavior Flip, a behavior management system that combines the best of restorative practices, PBIS, and MTSS to help build a culture of empathy, responsibility, and growth mindset

"In *Educate the Heart*, Jennifer Lee Quattrucci captures the true essence of what an authentic learning experience should be for a child. Loaded with turn key strategies, *Educate the Heart* serves as an instructional cookbook for authentic learning. Creativity, passion, and purpose, this book is vital for any educator trying to develop the 21st century whole child learner."—Don Epps, Royster Middle School Principal, #ChasingGreatness

"*Educate the Heart: Screen-Free Activities for Grades Pre-K–6 to Inspire Authentic Learning*, by Jennifer Lee Quattrucci, is a must have! Because our world has become so technology driven, some educators may struggle with finding ways to keep students engaged without screens. In this book, Jennifer provides several, practical activities that teachers can implement tomorrow in their classrooms. Although student engagement is necessary, we can't accomplish that goal without meeting the social and emotional needs of students. Jennifer addresses this topic and emphasizes its importance with her attention to kindness and community in the classroom. After reading this book, you will walk away encouraged and ignited, ready to make an impact in the lives of students."—Jimmy Baker, instructor, College of Education and Elementary Teacher

Educate the Heart

Screen-Free Activities for Grades PreK-6 to Inspire Authentic Learning

Jennifer Lee Quattrucci

ROWMAN & LITTLEFIELD
Lanham • Boulder • New York • London

Published by Rowman & Littlefield
An imprint of The Rowman & Littlefield Publishing Group, Inc.
4501 Forbes Boulevard, Suite 200, Lanham, Maryland 20706
www.rowman.com

6 Tinworth Street, London SE11 5AL

Copyright © 2019 by Jennifer Lee Quattrucci

All rights reserved. No part of this book may be reproduced in any form or by any electronic or mechanical means, including information storage and retrieval systems, without written permission from the publisher, except by a reviewer who may quote passages in a review.

British Library Cataloguing in Publication Information Available

Library of Congress Cataloging-in-Publication Data

Names: Quattrucci, Jennifer Lee, 1973- author.
Title: Educate the heart : screen-free activities for grades prek-6 to inspire authentic learning / Jennifer Lee Quattrucci.
Description: Lanham : Rowman & Littlefield, [2019] | Includes bibliographical references.
Identifiers: LCCN 2019013096 (print) | LCCN 2019021846 (ebook) | ISBN 9781475851861 (electronic) | ISBN 9781475851847 (cloth : alk. paper) | ISBN 9781475851854 (pbk. : alk. paper)
Subjects: LCSH: Elementary school teaching. | Preschool teaching. | Creative activities and seat work. | Affective education.
Classification: LCC LB1555 (ebook) | LCC LB1555 .Q39 2019 (print) | DDC 372.1102—dc23
LC record available at https://lccn.loc.gov/2019013096

To our childhood selves, and to Angelina, William, and all the children who deserve the special, meaningful moments full of joy, love, and learning we want for them.

Contents

Foreword xiii

Preface xv

Acknowledgments xvii

Introduction xxiii

1 Promoting Peace: Fifteen Ways to Empower Students to Handle Conflict through Kindness 1

2 Empower Your Students with Collaborative Work Space: Implementing Flexible Seating Options 15

3 Let's Talk about Math!: Fifteen Literature-Based Opportunities for Respectful and Effective Mathematical Discourse 25

4 Collaborative and Meaningful Literacy Centers: Fifteen Opportunities for Students to Extend Their Learning in Creative and Challenging Ways 47

5 Adding Flavor: Easy Classroom Recipes that Build Community and Teach Essential Skills 79

6 Embracing STEM Education: Fifteen Collaborative Group Activities to Inspire Critical-Thinking Skills, Communication, and Creativity 95

7 The Power of the Author Study: Fifteen Shared Reading Experiences to Encourage Communication and Build Critical-Thinking Skills in Your Classroom 109

8 Self-Expression through Innovative Art Integration: Fifteen Worthwhile Collaborative Projects to Inspire Creativity in Your Units of Study	127
9 Let Them Move!: Fifteen Ways to Improve Physical Fitness, Support Academic Concepts, and Increase Authentic Learning	145
10 Lose the Clip Chart, Color Changer, and Sticker Chart: Fifteen Ways to Build Community with a Growth Mind-set Approach to Classroom Discipline	159
11 Homework—Make It Meaningful: Fifteen Ways to Keep Kids Engaged and Encourage Authentic Learning at Home	167
12 The Communities Beyond Your Classroom Community: Fifteen Ways to Build Relationships that Support Meaningful Learning	175
Appendix: Book List	185
About the Author	197

Foreword

I believe that I often bring out the best in somebody's talents.
—David Bowie

One of my most favorite and memorable classroom activities as a young student was to build a catapult that fired paper balls across the room. I still cannot remember if we were studying medieval times, forces, or even pulleys and gears, but the project was so incredible that it left an impact on me that I still feel almost thirty years later. If my memory serves me, it was working with my father on the project that made it so special, not just the curriculum content, and that we were making a weapon. It was real. It was hands on. It was fun! To think, people actually built these things in real life and used them in battle!

Jennifer Quattrucci has compiled a magnificent gem of a resource that I wish I had had as a new teacher, and thankfully now, as a veteran teacher! As an advocate for STEM, STEAM, computational thinking, and accessible learning, I find Jenn's ideas for engaging students without using a device incredibly refreshing. Twenty-first-century education is often branded as something that requires electricity, while every aspect of collaboration, creativity, and critical thinking is apparent and relevant in the lessons throughout this book.

Against the backdrop of the ever-growing use of automation and edu-babble about preparing students for the future, Jenn reminds us to be empathetic. She emphasizes the importance of kindness, the beauty of mathematics, and the aesthetics of good writing without always staring at a screen. Not only can we engage modern learners, but we can also support parents in doing so at home with a plethora of activities.

While the lessons and activities mentioned throughout this book focus on different content areas, the theme remains consistent: education is about people. We are in the people business. Education is about empathy, collaboration, and community building. I may never have been a student in Jennifer's class, but I am incredibly envious of those who were and are.

The real 1:1 is more about building a relationship with every student in your class and less about the number of devices you have access to. Jennifer has done a fantastic job of showing how we can reach everyone—all learners—without using a screen. With multiple entry points, scaffolding tips, and differentiated instruction at the forefront, you will find yourself immersed in this book and excited to return to your classroom to teach, learn with, and continue to build rapport with your own students.

Brian Aspinall
Educator, three-time TEDx speaker, coder, consultant, and
author of *Code Breaker: Increase Creativity, Remix Assessment, and Develop a Class of Coder Ninjas!* and *Block Breaker: Building Knowledge and Amplifying Student Voice One Block at a Time*

Preface

Education is not the learning of facts but the training of the mind to think.
—Albert Einstein

The idea of a curriculum that makes the social and emotional learning needs of students a priority and ensures that all children are taught to think critically, collaborate effectively, communicate respectfully, and express themselves creatively has been my vision for many years. In a world where children are rushed from place to place, often occupied by devices, we as educators and parents need to create an environment where they are given time and allowed to focus, think, create, and learn.

Giving children the love they need and the time to develop competence is critical to their overall development. The ideas, activities, and lesson plans in this book cater to the well-being of the whole child. This book provides a framework full of hands-on, practical, and engaging opportunities that will empower students to handle conflict through kindness, implement effective and meaningful mathematical discourse, and extend their learning in all academic subjects in creative and challenging ways.

I have always used literature as an essential part of my curriculum and have found many ways to connect it with other subjects and skills. There are a great deal of award-winning children's books suggested and celebrated within these chapters. Author studies, literacy centers, classroom recipes, collaborative art projects, and mathematical problem solving are all greatly enhanced when beautiful books are meaningfully integrated.

STEM education is embraced with collaborative group activities to inspire critical-thinking skills, communication, and creativity. There are also many ways to improve physical fitness, which will also support academic concepts and increase authentic learning, included in this book.

In *Educate the Heart: Screen-Free Activities for Grades PreK–6 to Inspire Authentic Learning*, there are practical suggestions to make flexible seating work in any classroom, which will allow teachers and students to make the most of any collaborative work space, maximizing comfort and learning for all. This book addresses the topic of discipline with a growth mind-set approach, forgoing traditional reward/punishment systems and replacing such methods with practical and meaningful relationship-building tactics that balance lots of love and support with good common sense.

Every idea, activity, and strategy has been chosen with Aristotle's philosophy of "educating the mind without educating the heart is no education at all" at the core. I believe we can make a difference when we collectively agree and act on the knowledge that recognizing and managing emotions, maintaining positive cooperative relationships, being able to set and achieve positive goals, and learning to make responsible decisions are the most important lessons we can offer our children. All these skills are integrated in every subject in engaging and meaningful ways within the pages of this book.

> *Children are the world's most valuable resource and the best hope for the future. This compels us to invest in our nation's future, to consider and meet our obligations to our children and generations that will follow.*
> —John F. Kennedy

Acknowledgments

Community is first of all a quality of the heart. It grows from the spiritual knowledge that we are alive not for ourselves but for each other.
—Henri J. M. Nouwen

This book is the result of the inspiration, support, encouragement, and guidance of many outstanding individuals. It would not have been possible nor as meaningful without the following people, and I'm grateful for each and every one of them.

My parents, Ron and Alessandra Cece, have always supported my dream to be a teacher and have been there for every moment, big or small, in my teaching career. I'm grateful for their constant love and guidance and their willingness to help out in any way possible, whether it is helping me set up another new classroom, baking pink cupcakes for my students (Mom), or taking pictures for my first published book (Dad)!

My editor, Sarah Jubar, is the most inspiring, talented, and positive superwoman I have ever been blessed with the opportunity to work with. I truly appreciate her kindness and skill, and her expertise and ability to communicate her ideas in such a cheerful, constructive way made this entire book-writing process a sheer delight.

Sean Gaillard, the author of the wonderful masterpiece *The Pepper Effect* and founder of the Celebrate Monday and Trend the Positive movements, has been an inspiring and supportive friend. His enthusiasm for my idea and his sincere, heartfelt advice will always be remembered and appreciated.

Steve Harper is known to many as the Chief Rippler or @Rippleon because of his marvelous commitment to inspiring so many to make a difference each and every day. He shares his powerful message in *The Ripple Effect*, and I will forever be grateful that I took advantage of his ninety-day Virtual Ripple Program and that he has been my virtual coach for both my personal and professional life. Steve has helped and supported me through a multitude of experiences and situations and has encouraged me to go above and beyond what is expected, causing, well, ripples of happiness! I don't believe I would have ever thought it was possible to become a published author and be able to share my ideas with so many if it wasn't for the Virtual Ripple Program and having Steve as a coach.

Brian Aspinall leaves me speechless with his never-ending enthusiasm for creating the best possible environments and experiences for children everywhere. He sets the standard high for all educators, and his passion for bettering the world leaves me wanting to do more and do everything better! He not only motivates me and so many others with his high-energy commitment to quality education but also makes everything accessible with his ability to convey his ideas and methods with ease and with a huge dose of pure fun. It's an honor to call him my friend. His support of my ideas and help every step of the way has been a blessing. I'm humbled by the thoughtful and amazing foreword he cheerfully provided, making this book an even more special and meaningful endeavor.

Jeffrey Kubiak has spent so much time reading, editing, offering sincere and constructive advice, and encouraging me to not give up! He has been an amazing friend and cheerleader and is an awesome model of how to lead by example. His work devoted to kindness and compassion shows us that we are all in this together and can make a positive impact with one drop of kindness, which is also the title of his forthcoming children's book.

I am forever indebted to the talented Doug Campbell, author of *Essential Tips for Classroom Success* and *Discipline without Anger*, for taking an interest in my work and making me believe that, yes, I can be an author too! He also kept me on track throughout the process, always encouraging me to stay true to myself. It means so much to have his sincere endorsement.

It's been a pleasure to get to know and have the support of "The Zen Teacher" himself, Dan Tricarico. He helps teachers reduce stress and improve self-care and has certainly been a breath of fresh air as he read, offered great feedback on, and even decided to endorse this book.

Scott Allison—a professor of psychology who promotes leadership, heroism, overcoming adversity, and spreading kindness—has been both an inspiration and a supportive friend. His work in heroism and his desire to spread the word about how important it is to serve others at whatever cost is incomparable. It's an honor to call him my friend, and I appreciate all his positivity, the time and effort he put into reading my first drafts, and his excitement about endorsing the finished work.

The amazing author of the children's book *Everyone Can Learn Math*, Alice Aspinall, has been a pleasure to get to know and share ideas with. Because I am forever inspired by the work she does, encouraging parents to talk math with their children and her commitment to promoting a growth mind-set, her willingness to read my work and her wonderful endorsement is greatly appreciated.

Dave Schmittou, author of *It's Like Riding a Bike* and the forthcoming masterpiece *Bold Humility*, certainly deserves a huge "thank you very much" for somehow finding the time (he is currently training for the Boston Marathon!) to read my little book and being so enthusiastic about endorsing it. His dedication to teaching what matters and leading by example is inspiring to say the absolute least!

I've been a fan of Stefanie Hohl and her ABC See Hear Do series for quite some time now. She is a mom of five and is talented at creating meaningful learning experiences to ensure children are having fun while they learn. I was pleased that Stefanie took the time to read my work and extremely happy that she found it worthy to endorse. Her sincere words are truly appreciated.

Without Brian Mendler, I just don't know what the world of education would be like. He is truly changing lives, one teacher and student at a time. His book *That ONE Kid: Changing Lives, One Student at a Time* has forever changed the way I think about classroom management, and his daily messages on social media continue to motivate me to be that teacher who makes a difference by caring, building relationships, embracing criticism, and never taking things personally. I appreciate his time and attention to this book, and I'm humbled by his beautiful endorsement.

I am so grateful to have connected with Nathan Maynard. His work on social emotional learning and his dedication to building a better school climate through relationships is remarkable. I learned so much from having the privilege to read an advance copy of his recently released book *Hacking School Discipline*, and I appreciate the time and effort he put into reading my chapters and offering valuable feedback. I really appreciate how kind he was in every single comment and helpful tip he gave me to improve my work. His endorsement means so much because I know he is passionate about inspiring authentic learning and really reaching the hearts of all students.

Jimmy Baker is a powerful educator who I have had the pleasure to learn from for years. His straightforward yet imaginative methods of reaching young children, matched with his enthusiasm and huge heart, inspire me to be a better teacher. He graciously took the time to read and offer feedback on this book, and I am grateful to have his amazing support.

I am fortunate to work with dedicated professionals in the city of Providence. Alex Lucini is an outstanding music teacher at West Broadway Middle School who also takes time to read motivational storybooks to kindergarten classrooms. He is also the dad of two beautiful elementary school children, and it means so much to me that he found the advance copy of my book worthwhile and decided to endorse it. I am so appreciative of his support.

Acknowledgments

I've known Edda Cambio Carmadello since we were in college together studying to be teachers. Throughout the years, in everything she's done, she has always been a positive force and a game changer. From her days running the summer program at the Silver Lake Annex Center to being an amazing middle school teacher and then phenomenal principal to her current role as executive director of specialized services for Providence schools, she has made a huge impact on so many. Her belief in all I am trying to do with my students and her support for this book has truly meant so much.

I must acknowledge and thank Blake Rocha and Kristi D'Amore, who both work with me at Harry Kizirian Elementary School and have been so kind, encouraging, and truly the best cheerleaders throughout this writing process.

Jannine Maynard, Ashley Marie Young, and Donna Corvese have been awesome all these months, asking about the book, listening to all my ideas, and believing it was all going to happen! I'm thankful for their support and friendship always.

West Shaw is a seventh-grade AVID leadership teacher in Las Vegas, Nevada, forthcoming author, and really great friend. He has been supportive of my ideas and work throughout this entire process. He is one of the first people who suggested I write a book to help teachers after we worked together on a DonorsChoose project. I'm so grateful for his motivation and encouragement.

Dom Baza has been a wonderful and supportive friend throughout the years, encouraging me to always shoot for the stars. We started our blogs around the same time, focusing on fashion, hoping to inspire others to be themselves and not be afraid to be different. Throughout the years we have both grown, moved in different directions with our blogs and careers, and focused on the things that were most meaningful to us, always searching for ways we could make a difference. Dom has supported my classroom as a generous and enthusiastic contributor to the DonorsChoose organization and wholeheartedly cheers me on as I try my best to do what's right and make sure my students have what they need.

David West could not possibly be a more supportive friend. He believed in this book when it was all just an idea and has encouraged me every step of the way. I'm grateful for the sincere feedback and the enormous amount of time he spent listening to me go on and on and on about basically every chapter, every activity, every picture, and every quote. He was also able to help me put every doubt I ever had about this book to rest. He was there from start to finish, and I will always remember and appreciate his enthusiasm and encouragement.

I must acknowledge Richard Reo for his appreciation for quality teaching and education and his constant, sincere friendship. He always says that I'm the "happiest" teacher and loves hearing about the students and all that goes on in the classroom. His interest and recognition of all that I do motivates me to do more and has inspired me to share my ideas in this book.

Kristine Moore has been my best friend for more than thirty years and has been there through absolutely every part of my teaching career (and life)! We attended Classical High School together, and since then she has always been enthusiastic and supportive of everything I've done to become a better teacher throughout the years. When I told her I was thinking of writing a book full of teaching ideas and hands-on activities to motivate children to learn and express themselves creatively, she immediately said what a perfect idea it was and that she knew I could do it and that it would be great. She helped me out by reading and critiquing my very first attempt at my first chapter. Having her support truly means so much.

My husband and I met when I was a kindergarten teacher and he was the gym teacher at the old Asa Messer Annex in Providence, Rhode Island. He has always been amazed by the time and energy I put into my lessons and the way I work so hard to learn and grow as a teacher. Jim has been excited about this book since I first showed him the title and chapter list. He has done everything he possibly could to allow me all the time I needed to write. There is no way I would have been able to focus on my ideas and all the details involved in creating this book if it wasn't for Jim and all the things he took care of without ever complaining. I cannot possibly thank him enough for doing so much to make it easy for me to make this dream come true. His belief in my ideas, his faith in what I'm capable of, and his love mean everything.

My daughter, Angelina, and my son, William, deserve huge acknowledgments for their love, patience, and understanding while I've been consumed with my regular teacher work and this book. They listened to many screen-free ideas and gave their honest opinions about whether or not they were "fun enough" for the book. Without their support, love, and sweetness, this book would definitely not have been possible.

Introduction

Educating the mind without educating the heart is no education at all.
—Aristotle

Throughout the pages of *Educate the Heart: Screen-Free Activities for Grades PreK–6 to Inspire Authentic Learning in Your Classroom*, you will discover a wealth of ideas and activities specifically designed for the early childhood or elementary school teacher who is passionate about influencing the ways students think, learn, and grow as individuals.

Every screen-free idea, strategy, suggestion, and method in this book is based on the belief that every child is an individual and should be in an environment where he or she is given time and allowed to focus, think, create, and learn. Each chapter is full of ideas that can be immediately implemented and adapted to fit in with any preK–6 classroom setting and within any set curriculum or framework. The activities don't require any fancy or expensive equipment and are sure to keep all students engaged, happy, and motivated to keep on learning!

The ideas in each chapter can be implemented in any order or sequence and at any time of the year. They provide opportunities to build critical-thinking skills, encourage communication, and inspire creativity while empowering students to master important academic concepts and skills. Busy teachers will be happy to see that the activities are carefully organized by subject and skill and that the materials required are clearly listed. There are more than two hundred wonderful literature suggestions for teachers to connect with the wide variety of activities found throughout each chapter.

The book focuses on fostering a growth mind-set in STEM and mathematical discourse and on utilizing best practices for encouraging children to reflect, improve, and effectively collaborate. The topics of effective classroom management and discipline are clearly discussed and approached with thoughtful, respectful methods for establishing relationships and building community. Flexible seating is explained and made practical to make the most of any work space and to accommodate the needs of all students.

There are fifteen detailed collaborative STEM challenges that not only embrace science, technology, engineering, and math learning but are also designed to inspire critical-thinking skills, communication, and creativity. Mathematical discourse is explained with practical methods for implementing and encouraging it effectively at every age level, with examples for multiple skills and tasks.

Teachers will find fifteen complete literacy center ideas full of meaningful opportunities for students to extend their learning in creative and challenging ways. The centers are designed to cater to students of varied abilities and learning styles and will enhance any reading program. Adding one center or implementing all of them throughout the year will add many opportunities for authentic learning, independent thinking, and decision making within a classroom. The simple literacy centers found in this book are easy for teachers to put together and will surely strengthen the reading, writing, and communication skills of students in the most engaging way.

Author studies help classrooms form close connections through shared reading experiences. In this book there are a wide variety of unique shared reading experiences that will allow classrooms to celebrate fifteen different authors and encourage students to think in innovative ways. Students are encouraged to read and respond to books and to improve critical-thinking skills as they compare and contrast themes, analyze text and illustrations, and make personal connections between an author's life and work and their own life and work. Authors become writing mentors for readers as they read and respond to exceptional literature in a variety of ways.

The fifteen literature-based recipes and fifteen collaborative art projects are arranged in a simple-to-follow format with easy and affordable materials listed, clear instructions, and many helpful tips for successful implementation. Teachers will find that the fifteen ways to improve physical fitness while supporting academic concepts are both practical and beneficial to the overall well-being of their students. Each fun movement idea is meant to keep students active and engaged while learning without requiring an enormous amount of prep or fancy equipment.

Homework can be meaningful for all students when it is thoughtfully assigned and when students are allowed to be creative, work at their own pace, and make choices. The fifteen ideas in the homework chapter are appropriate ways for students to continue learning authentically when they are not in school and can be adapted to fit in with any grade level or curriculum. These ideas are meant to be the actual homework, not extra work and assignments for families to participate in after already completing worksheets, endless math problems, and other traditional homework assignments.

Community is an important part of educating the heart of a child. We need to teach children that we are all here for each other, and we need to lead by example. There are fifteen ways to build relationships that support meaningful learning shared in this book that will make it easy for educators to connect with communities outside the classroom in powerful ways.

Every chapter and every idea within each chapter was chosen as a meaningful way to break away from technology and inspire authentic learning. Teachers and students will appreciate the imaginative, hands-on approach in this book and be grateful for the experienced advice and practicality of each and every activity.

Chapter One

Promoting Peace

Fifteen Ways to Empower Students to Handle Conflict through Kindness

> Peace is not the absence of conflict. It is the ability to handle conflict by peaceful means.
>
> —Ronald Reagan

Classroom teachers have the power to affect the ways in which students view and handle conflict. The activities and strategies in this chapter are designed to help students learn to speak, act, and react with understanding, self-control, and respect for themselves and others. These activities will build students' confidence in their ability to solve and prevent problems. As teachers implement these simple yet effective ideas, they will empower students with peacemaking skills. Teachers will help children learn how to identify their feelings and express them in ways that promote understanding and peaceful conflict resolution.

PROMOTING PEACE STRATEGY 1: KNOWLEDGE IS POWER

Materials

- *In My Heart: A Book of Feelings* (Growing Hearts) by Jo Witek (Harry N. Abrams, 2014)

    Feelings are at the root of conflict and confrontation. When in conflict, people will feel afraid, angry, confused, or frustrated. Recognizing and acknowledging these emotions is the first step toward handling them ap-

propriately. Children must be able to identity their feelings in order to express them in ways that promote understanding and peaceful resolution. As students come to realize and respect their own feelings, they will feel less threatened by others and more confident in managing their own reactions to conflict.
- Chart paper and markers
- Writing supplies such as paper, pencils, and crayons
- Poster board or book-making supplies (paper, stapler, hole puncher, etc.) as optional choices for collaborative project

Directions

Teachers should begin this activity by discussing where feelings come from and what they look like. It's great to start with a picture book, and there are many available for children of all ages on this topic. Because of the vast selection out there, it's important to choose books wisely when building lessons around them. *In My Heart: A Book of Feelings* (Growing Hearts) by Jo Witek (Harry N. Abrams, 2014) is a wonderful book for introducing and discussing feelings for all ages because the illustrations and descriptions are simple yet perfect for each feeling described. The main character is fun, playful, and easy for both boys and girls to relate to.

To help students identify basic emotions, teachers should read the story and then ask the children to recall the feelings mentioned in the book. Teachers can then chart the responses and ask students to brainstorm and add adjectives that describe their own emotions to the list. Students might think of words such as *happy, sad, angry, excited, proud, guilty, embarrassed, sorry, lonely, bored, tired, loving, surprised, afraid, silly, worried, disappointed, content,* and *impatient.*

Teachers can give students paper, pencils, and crayons and ask them to create faces to represent several of the emotions on the list. Teachers should encourage students to think about what might have caused the emotions and share their ideas. Once students have had the opportunity to think about and share their ideas about feelings, teachers should help students understand that feelings come from inside a person as a response to thoughts, actions, or events.

It's a great idea for teachers to assign partners or small groups of students a different feeling to discuss and ask them to record the different times they may have felt that emotion. Each group or set of partners can create a poster or book devoted to their assigned feeling. Displaying the posters in the classroom and arranging the books in a classroom library make the experience meaningful and create an environment that inspires authentic learning.

PROMOTING PEACE STRATEGY 2:
THANKS FOR THE "HEADS-UP"!

Materials

- Chart paper, markers
- Writing supplies such as paper, pencils, and crayons

Directions

Teachers can help students recognize signs of emotions in their bodies. They can begin by making a two-column chart on chart paper. The left column should be labeled "Feelings" and the right column "What Happens?" The students and teachers should come up with six to eight feelings together and then list them in the left column. Teachers then ask students to tell them how their body feels as they experience each emotion. Students might say when they are sad they want to cry and when they are mad they feel hot or have a stomachache.

Students can make their own mini version of the chart to take home. Teachers can then ask them to pay attention to their bodies throughout the day and evening. When they experience one of the feelings listed, they should notice how their body responds and write it on the chart. The next day their observations can be compiled and added to the class chart.

Students should be guided in brainstorming ways they can use the signs from their bodies as a "heads-up" to help them react to a conflict in a peaceful way. For example, students who know that anger makes them feel like they have extra energy can make use of that energy with just their hands by making two fists and then throwing them open as if they were tossing their angry feelings away. Teachers should encourage students to talk nicely to themselves when they know these feelings are coming, saying things like "I can calm down" or "I can explain how I feel and get help." These ideas can be added to the class chart in bold colors so students will quickly be able to find them when their body is giving them a "heads-up."

PROMOTING PEACE STRATEGY 3:
COLORS SPEAK LOUDER THAN WORDS

Materials

- *The Color Monster: A Story about Emotions* by Anna Zlenas (Little, Brown Books for Young Readers, 2018)
- *My Many Colored Days* by Dr. Seuss (Knopf, 1996)

- Recording of "I've Got the Blues, Greens, and Reds" by Tom Chapin
- Paper and colorful art supplies such as crayons, markers, or paint

Directions

Colors are powerful in evoking and representing feelings. Using literature and song will help children understand this connection. Teachers can read aloud picture books that connect feelings and colors, such as *The Color Monster: A Story about Emotions* by Anna Zlenas (Little, Brown Books for Young Readers, 2018) and *My Many Colored Days* by Dr. Seuss (Knopf, 1996). They can also share singer Tom Chapin's "I've Got the Blues, Greens, and Reds" and give students paper and crayons, markers, or paint and encourage them to use color to show different emotions. The creations can be displayed and used as a springboard for discussion. Children can guess and discuss which emotion each drawing or painting represents.

PROMOTING PEACE STRATEGY 4: ACTIONS SPEAK LOUDER THAN WORDS

Materials

- Index cards or small pieces of paper
- Marker or pen

Directions

A quick, simple, and effective way to help children become more confident in identifying and expressing different emotions is to play feeling charades. Teachers can use index cards or small pieces of paper to make emotion cards. On each card, write the name of an emotion (happy, disappointed, annoyed, and so on). Teachers should then ask a student volunteer to choose a card and act out the emotion written on it. They should explain that, rather than using words, the students should act out the emotion through facial expressions and body language. For example, they can try frowning, yawning, or jumping up and down. Other students need to guess and explain what emotion they think is being acted out and why.

PROMOTING PEACE STRATEGY 5:
IF YOU CAN'T THINK OF SOMETHING KIND TO SAY, YOU ARE NOT THINKING HARD ENOUGH

Materials

- Chart paper
- Marker

Directions

Teachers should always lead by example by speaking and acting with kindness. In times of conflict, kind words and actions are often neglected in favor of harsh ones. Teachers can help students build a vocabulary of kind words by constantly modeling considerate language and encouraging students to avoid saying words that are hurtful to others. Teachers can also keep an ongoing chart of new and interesting kind words children find to empower them with many options.

PROMOTING PEACE STRATEGY 6:
SPEAK WITH VELVET WORDS

Materials

- Blocks
- Velvet
- Sandpaper

Directions

Teachers will enjoy giving students hands-on experience with the "texture" of words. They can explain and show how some words are soft to the listener while others are abrasive and rough. To help teach the concept of positive and negative language, teachers should cover one block with velvet and another with sandpaper. As students feel the textures and talk about how words feel like velvet and sandpaper, they realize that their own words can be comforting or abrasive to others.

PROMOTING PEACE STRATEGY 7: COMPASSION BLOOMS WHERE IT'S PLANTED

Materials

- Sticky notes, blank index cards, or postcards
- Colorful pens or markers

Directions

Compassion can be taught in simple and effective ways. It's easy for teachers to model compassion by complimenting students on their successes, asking about their day or weekend activities, and being sure to address bullying behaviors in a timely and consistent manner. Many teachers use positive affirmations every morning and throughout the day so students are sure that they are appreciated and reminded of their unique qualities and talents.

Teachers can prepare different types of notes and cards to always have ready and available. Some ideas for affirmations are "You are awesome," "You can do whatever you focus on," "You are creative," and "You are loved." Note cards, pencils, and other stationery items with positive messages on them are readily available, and they are great, but it's even better if teachers can take the time to write their own personalized and meaningful messages on sticky notes, index cards, or actual postcards, which are very affordable when purchased in bulk.

Many teachers also create affirmations for themselves and other teachers as reminders of how important they are. A simple message of "I make a difference one student at a time," "My students deserve my best," or "My job matters!" may be just what teachers need to remind them of their purpose on a challenging day.

PROMOTING PEACE STRATEGY 8: TREE OF KINDNESS

Materials

- Construction paper or card stock
- Art supplies such as scissors, glue, markers, and crayons

Directions

Teachers and students can create a tree out of construction paper or card stock for an interactive bulletin board display that they can transform throughout the year. In September, when students are caught being kind, they can add apples with sentences on them describing the acts of kindness. In October, a pumpkin patch can be created under the tree, and sentences about acts of kindness can be written on the pumpkins. In November, colorful fall leaves would make a beautiful addition to display the "kind act" sentences.

Many classrooms are very creative with their kindness trees and allow them to represent themes and units of study they are working on. A penguin theme can be integrated by adding a pond of ice and penguins. Chapter books can be celebrated by re-creating scenes from a shared read aloud with the Tree of Kindness in the background. One classroom teacher read *Charlotte's Web* by E. B. White (HarperCollins, 2012) and wrote the acts of kindness on farm animals.

When creating and adding to a classroom Tree of Kindness, it's important that teachers and students discuss each act of kindness that the apple, pumpkin, or leaf is being added for and the impact it has had on the class. For example, "Angelina noticed that a teacher had her hands full and was having trouble opening the door, so she held the door open for her." The students should be asked why it was considered a kind thing to do, how they think the teacher felt, and how Angelina felt.

Some teachers have used this as an individual activity, assigning one "apple" or other object or even a container to each child, but to truly build community and instill desirable social skills, this should be a group effort. The class, including teachers and paraprofessionals, should work together to create an atmosphere of peace, not create a competition to see who will have the most kind acts displayed.

PROMOTING PEACE STRATEGY 9: COMMUNICATION LEADS TO COMMUNITY

Materials

- None

Directions

It's important to give students the tools they need for active listening. When people communicate effectively, conflict can often be prevented or resolved. Teachers need to explain to children that communication involves both speaking and listening and ask children to think of ways they can be good listeners. Their ideas can then be written on a chart to display in the classroom.

Teachers can guide students by sharing and role-playing important active listener traits. Students should realize that an active listener needs to focus attention on the speaker by stopping what they are doing and looking at the speaker. Active listening requires acknowledgment to the speaker that they understand by nodding or responding briefly ("I see . . . yes . . . I understand . . . ") so the speaker knows they are listening.

Students should know that an active listener should try not to interrupt because it is impolite and may cause the speaker to lose his or her train of thought. Active listening involves paraphrasing when appropriate. Children should be taught to repeat the speaker's ideas or message in their own words. This will ensure the speaker knows the listener has understood what he or she is saying. It's important to teach children that active listeners truly listen and do not try to tell the speaker what to do unless asked to do so.

PROMOTING PEACE STRATEGY 10: MAGNIFY THEIR STRENGTHS

Materials

- Construction paper

- Craft paper or poster board
- Art supplies such as markers, crayons, and glue

Directions

Teachers can celebrate one student each week by creating a class compliment quilt in their honor. At the beginning of the year, teachers should assign each student a week during which he or she will be the subject of a compliment quilt. The order can be determined alphabetically, or students can choose numbers during the first week of school. A calendar should be posted with the order and assignments to eliminate student anticipation.

Each week, teachers can ask the children to think of something they appreciate about the celebrated student. Compliments might include "William is friendly to everyone and helpful. He taught me how to tie my shoe at recess" or "Dante is creative. He made a really cool design during art yesterday."

Students should each be given a colorful eight-by-eight-inch square of paper. They need to write the compliment on it and draw a picture to go with it. All the squares can be glued on a large sheet of craft paper or poster board. The quilt can be hung up and displayed for the rest of the week and then sent home as a keepsake for the celebrated student.

PROMOTING PEACE STRATEGY 11: CREATE A WIN-WIN SITUATION

Materials

- None

Directions

When conflict does occur, students need to know that there are many ways to deal with it. They can try to look for a win-win solution. To solve problems in a way that meets the needs of everyone involved, students must be taught to study the problems carefully. They must identify the needs of each person. Teachers can have students practice studying problems to find win-win solutions daily. For example, if two children are having difficulty sharing a toy, perhaps they could agree to a certain amount of time each child gets to spend with it so that they both feel it's fair. If two children are sharing a storage space for school supplies, they could discuss ways to arrange things so it's easier and comfortable for them.

Teachers should involve the whole class in coming up with kind ways to make everyone happy depending on each particular conflict. Students should

be encouraged to think of themselves as problem solvers when problems arise with other children. This will help them develop the habit of thinking of what others need and want and not just what they want. Students will be naturally kind to others and seek ways to make everyone happy with kindness.

PROMOTING PEACE STRATEGY 12: HOW I FEEL MATTERS

Materials

- Chart paper
- Markers

Directions

A great way to teach students how to be assertive and stand up for themselves is to explain and encourage "I-messages." Each person needs to state how he or she feels about a situation and explain what he or she needs. No one is allowed to be rough or forceful, and no one is allowed to retreat. To introduce I-messages, it's best for teachers to give students patterns and examples to use as models for their own messages. Having the patterns visible and accessible to all is important so students will immediately be able to use an I-message when needed. A few examples that teachers can write on an anchor chart are "I feel _____ when you _____ because _____," "I _____ when you _____ because _____," "I _____ when you _____ and I would like _____."

Teachers can help students gain confidence in using these patterns by giving them practice scenarios to respond to with I-messages. Many teachers allow their students to practice responding to conflicts they have observed in their classroom. For example, Quin took Isobel's markers without asking. What should Isobel say to Quin? Students should be guided to come up with an I-message such as "I don't like it when you take my markers without asking, and I would like you to ask me next time."

PROMOTING PEACE STRATEGY 13: IMAGINATION CHANGES EVERYTHING

Materials

- Table and tablecloth to create a simple theater
- Art supplies such as popsicle sticks, craft scraps, construction paper, movable eyes, and glue to create puppets

Directions

Children should be encouraged to use their imagination to help them adjust to new situations, express their feelings, and work through difficult challenges. Puppets allow students to have fun and practice their new communication skills and new ways of responding to conflict before they actually have to put them into practice. It's easy for teachers to set up a puppet theater without any special equipment. They can put a tablecloth over a table and create a theatrical atmosphere, encouraging creativity and freedom of expression.

Puppets are easy to make with popsicle sticks and any type of craft scraps or materials teachers happen to have. Construction paper, felt, tissue paper, yarn, movable eyes, glitter, sequins, and buttons all work well with regular school glue. Students can make puppets to represent themselves, fictional characters, or any creatures they imagine. It would be great for students to have time to use the puppets as a center activity and be encouraged to use them to resolve actual conflicts that happen during the day. Many teachers also use the puppets during whole group time and pretend a puppet has a problem he or she needs help with. Students love coming up with peaceful ideas to "help" the puppet resolve the conflict.

PROMOTING PEACE STRATEGY 14:
PEACE BEGINS WITH A SMILE

Materials

- Simple furniture such as a desk or small table and two chairs
- A cheerful tablecloth
- Feeling charts, I-message patterns, and anchor charts representing work and activities the class has engaged in regarding respectful speaking and active listening

Directions

Teachers can easily set up a peace corner where students can meet to solve problems. A table or desk covered with a cheerful tablecloth and two chairs in the corner of the room are all that is needed to start. Many teachers find it helpful to have I-message patterns, feeling charts, and reminders of the work and activities students have engaged in regarding respectful speaking and active listening nearby. Boundaries should be established, such as speaking in quiet voices, using peaceful language, and so on. One classroom has a quote by Mother Teresa hanging in the peace corner that states, "Peace begins with a smile."

PROMOTING PEACE STRATEGY 15:
CONSISTENCY IS EVERYTHING

Materials

- None

Directions

The best way for teachers to reinforce conflict resolution and promote peace and kindness is through consistent practice. The other activities in this chapter will build students' confidence in their ability to solve and prevent problems when implemented on a regular basis. Allowing time every day for students to talk about their feelings will give students the consistency they need so that the peaceful strategies they have learned will become a natural part of their everyday life.

> *When we can talk about our feelings, they become less overwhelming, less upsetting, and less scary.*
> —Fred Rogers

Chapter Two

Empower Your Students with Collaborative Work Space

Implementing Flexible Seating Options

> When a flower doesn't bloom you fix the environment in which it grows, not the flower.
>
> —Alexander Den Heijer

Students of all ages feel empowered by having some degree of choice and control over their learning environment. Flexible seating options allow students to choose where they want to work and with whom. It allows them the opportunity to change their location and position as needed. When students are given the freedom to make independent choices and solve problems in this way, they learn critical-thinking skills.

Flexible seating encourages students to share their space and supplies and provides them with opportunities to take turns in different locations. This is different from having traditional desks, which can be very restricting and may make students feel territorial or possessive over their belongings and assigned spots. When teachers implement flexible seating options, they create a learning environment that reflects that of the real world.

Educating the heart of a child requires that all the student's social and emotional needs are met prior to academic instruction. Meeting these needs will ensure that authentic, meaningful learning can take place. If students are uncomfortable, they will most likely be distracted and unproductive. A seat that is comfortable for one child will not necessarily be the best one for another student. Providing students with flexible seating choices will empower each child to make the important decision of how and where he or she can learn best and how to get along respectfully within his or her classroom community.

All teachers know how important it is for students to be moving throughout the day. Providing students with a variety of seating options not only improves their comfort and empowers them to have the freedom to choose, but is also beneficial to their physical health. Flexible seating allows them to bounce, wobble, rock, lean, or stand, which increases oxygen flow to the brain, circulation, and core strength. Students are also able to burn more calories and increase their metabolism. When students have the opportunity to move their body when they feel a need to, their minds are more focused and alert.

Many flexible seating options stimulate students' sense of touch. Some students, such as those on the autism spectrum, are high-sensory seekers. Children who are sensory seekers should be given the outlet they need to regulate their body so they can be relaxed or calm. Providing sensory stimulating seating options is a safe way to help these students focus and process information in the nurturing environment of their own classroom.

Cooperative and collaborative work is greatly enhanced with flexible seating. Having a variety of options will allow students to quickly and easily pair up, work in small groups, and have whole-class discussions without anyone having to move heavy furniture around to establish and maintain eye contact.

A classroom community that prioritizes communication, cooperation, respect, and kindness will thrive when flexible seating options are implemented effectively. The result will be authentic collaboration, enhanced creativity, and better communication.

It's crucial for teachers to establish effective classroom management tools when beginning to add flexible seating options to their classrooms. With careful organization and a systematic plan, flexible seating can be implemented in a fair and nondisruptive way. Every seating option should have its own clear set of expectations, and these expectations should be stated and accessible at all times. Each seating option described in this chapter has its own suggested set of student expectations that can be written on an anchor chart and posted in the classroom.

Teachers who have had success utilizing flexible seating know it is important to have a consistent routine when giving students the opportunity to choose their own seat and space. One effective and fair way is to allow students to choose their seats for the following day before they leave at the end of the day. To ensure that everyone has an opportunity to pick first, teachers can make their way through the class alphabetically.

Many teachers ask students to sign a contract promising to use the work spaces appropriately. The contract will state that the student promises to choose a seat that will allow him or her to work well and respect the students and supplies in the area. The contract will also state the understanding that if the student does not follow the rules, he or she will have to move to a spot the teacher thinks will better meet his or her needs.

It's important for teachers to communicate the purpose and guidelines of flexible seating options to the students' families. They should be informed about the benefits and expectations of the implementation. Families should know what types of seating are available and how the students will be supported in making their seating choices. They are often very appreciative of the options available for their children and will even donate new or gently used furniture to the classroom!

FLEXIBLE SEATING OPTION 1: LAP DESK TRAYS

Benefits

Lap desks and lap desk trays are affordable and can be found at many stores and on a great number of websites. Many options have folding legs that make them easy to pack up and store. They are great for extending activities to the outdoors and for students to take when visiting another room in the school. Many lap desks also have storage compartments built in to keep supplies accessible and organized.

Student Expectations

- Find a good working spot.
- Do not lean on tray to stand.
- Make sure markings do not get on the tray.
- Stay in one spot.

FLEXIBLE SEATING OPTION 2: SCOOP ROCKER CHAIRS

Benefits

Scoop rocker chairs are great for students to read and relax in and can often be found in affordable sets of six. They sit at floor level and come in a variety of colors. They are a very practical flexible seating option because of their portability and because they can be easily cleaned and quickly stacked.

Student Expectations

- Find a good working spot.
- Do not lean back too far.

- Stay one arm's length away from others.
- Stay in one spot.

FLEXIBLE SEATING OPTION 3: WOBBLE STOOLS

Benefits

Wobble stools are great for keeping children of all ages in motion, engaging their core and back muscles, and working their legs and arms. Unlike regular chairs that allow children to slouch and encourage poor posture that will cause back problems later in life, wobble stools ensure that students maintain good posture while naturally engaging their core for stronger, healthier backs. The stools are designed to rock and never tip over. Nonslip rubberized bottoms allow students to teeter, totter, jiggle, and sway all day long without any fear of the stool slipping from underneath them. Cushioned tops keep students comfortable even if they do need to sit in a certain spot for a long period.

Student Expectations

- Find a good working spot.
- Only sit on the stool.
- Rock gently back and forth only.
- Stay in one spot.

FLEXIBLE SEATING OPTION 4: BEANBAG SEATS

Benefits

Beanbag seats are a very cozy flexible seating option and easy for students to move around in. They provide excellent relaxation for students who are prone to experience anxiety and depression. Beanbag seats with vinyl covers are a necessity in the classroom so they can be easily wiped clean. They are best when they also have double-stitched seams, smooth edges, and double zippers to keep the beads safely inside.

Student Expectations

- Find a good working spot.
- Only sit or lie on the seat.
- Never stand on the beanbag seat.
- Stay in one spot.

FLEXIBLE SEATING OPTION 5: STABILITY BALLS

Benefits

Stability balls encourage students to learn and practice healthy posture. Because a stability ball is not stable, students need to try to balance themselves on it. Coincidently, the perfect spinal posture is the easiest to balance with. Because of this, a child's body will automatically try to align itself with the proper posture. A stability ball will cause a student to change positions often to balance. This helps reduce damage caused by prolonged sitting in the same position.

Student Expectations

- Find a good working spot.
- Only bounce gently.
- No standing or spinning.
- Do not bump into others.
- Stay in one spot.

FLEXIBLE SEATING OPTION 6: WIGGLE SEATS

Benefits

Wiggle seats, or sensory cushions as they are sometimes called, are wonderful tools to help students stay focused by allowing for subtle movements without calling attention to wiggling. Sensory cushions can come in different textures (bumpy, smooth, spiky), sizes, and shapes. They are filled with air, and depending on the amount of wiggling needed, you can adjust the amount they are inflated to provide more or less "wiggle." Some wiggle cushions have a wedge shape that promotes good posture. They are especially great to use on the classroom carpet to define boundaries, and they are versatile enough to be used throughout the classroom without taking up a lot of space.

Student Expectations

- Find a good working spot.
- Only sit on the seat.
- Do not stand on the seat.
- Stay in one spot.

FLEXIBLE SEATING OPTION 7: YOGA MATS

Benefits

Yoga mats with high-density foam material comfortably cushion the spine, hips, knees, and elbows of students even when they need to be on a hard classroom floor. When they have moisture-resistant technology and are made from high-quality materials, they can be easily cleaned. Yoga mats are very easy to transport and store.

Student Expectations

- Find a good working spot.
- Stay on your own yoga mat.
- Make sure markings do not get on the mat.

FLEXIBLE SEATING OPTION 8: BEACH CHAIRS

Benefits

Beach chairs are often found at the end of summer at very affordable prices, which is wonderful for teachers wanting to add lightweight and comfortable seating options to their classrooms. They are often adjustable and very easy to clean. Beach chairs are also great for outdoor lessons and activities since they are created with the elements of nature in mind.

Student Expectations

- Find a good working spot.
- Do not bring any liquids to this spot.
- Keep your feet toward the ground.
- Stay in one spot.

FLEXIBLE SEATING OPTION 10: ROCKING CHAIRS

Benefits

Rocking chairs that are built to last and constructed with durable materials are a favorite seating choice for both teachers and students. It's important to add comfortable cushions that have removable covers for easy machine washing when adding rocking chairs to a classroom. Because there are so many different models and types available, taking the time to find a rocking chair, or several rocking chairs, that are well made and a good fit for a classroom is well worth the effort.

Student Expectations

- Find a good working spot.
- Only sit on the rocking chair.
- Rock gently back and forth.
- Stay in one spot.

FLEXIBLE SEATING OPTION 11: CAFÉ STOOLS

Benefits

Café stools are easy to transport and stackable for convenient storage. They are great for collaborative work, can easily fit around a table, and are affordable and easy to clean.

Student Expectations

- Choose a good working spot.
- Only sit on the seat.
- Do not rock back and forth on the stools.

- Stay in one spot.

FLEXIBLE SEATING OPTION 12: INDIVIDUAL RUG SPOTS

Benefits

Individual rug spots are a wonderful option because they are affordable, easy to clean, and can be used in any area to give students their own individual learning space. They come in many shapes and sizes, and often carpet stores will donate carpet square samples to classrooms if requested.

Student Expectations

- Choose a good working spot.
- Keep all materials in your area.
- Only one student is allowed per carpet.

- Stay in one spot.

FLEXIBLE SEATING OPTION 13: PUFFY CHAIRS

Benefits

Chairs that are very soft and have puffy cushions are super comfortable for students, and sitting in them may even make students feel that they are being cuddled. They are easy to move around in, and many can be folded for simple storage.

Student Expectations

- Choose a good working spot.
- Do not bring any liquids to this seat.
- Keep your feet toward the ground.
- Stay in one spot.

FLEXIBLE SEATING OPTION 14: SOFA/COUCH

Benefits

Having a sofa in a classroom that is committed to inspiring authentic learning is essential because students will find it to be just the right piece of furniture they need to gather for small group discussions, to collaborate on projects, or to share stories. A couch with an armless design is ideal to maximize the space, and many can be found with a vinyl finish for easy cleaning.

Student Expectations

- Choose a good working spot.
- Do not bring any liquids to this spot.
- Your feet must point toward the ground.
- Respect the personal space of others on the couch.
- Stay in one spot.

FLEXIBLE SEATING OPTION 15: STANDING DESKS

Benefits

A standing desk is a great flexible seating option for students who prefer to stand while they work. The small movements at standing desks, like fidgeting, can add up to a big difference when burning calories, helping students to stay physically fit and also increasing focus on the task at hand. When choosing to add standing desks to a classroom, it is crucial to find adjustable and durable models to maximize comfort and ensure safety for all students.

Student Expectations

- Find a good working seat.
- Keep all supplies on the desk.
- Be respectful of other students near you.
- Stay in one spot.

SUMMARY

An effective flexible seating implementation requires careful thought and planning. Teachers must establish a consistent and fair routine for choosing seats. Clear rules and expectations are critical and must be communicated to both students and their families. The transformation is so much more than just new furniture, and the positive impact it has on a classroom community proves it is well worth the time and effort.

Students in a classroom with effective flexible seating implementation will experience better comfort, many options for sensory input, improved behavior, better collaboration, and stronger social skills. Authentic learning will be inspired as students' needs are met and they are able to take responsibility for their own learning.

> *Learning is not the product of teaching. Learning is the product of the activity of learners.*
> —John Holt

Chapter Three

Let's Talk about Math!

*Fifteen Literature-Based Opportunities for
Respectful and Effective Mathematical Discourse*

> *Pure mathematics is, in its own way, the poetry of logical ideas.*
> —Albert Einstein

Wouldn't it be absolutely amazing to help children recognize the relevance and importance of math in their daily lives and to give them unique ways to interact as a community of learners? Of course! You want students to not only see math as a dynamic, enjoyable, and necessary part of their lives but also to be challenged in a nurturing environment, encouraged to persevere, and ultimately cultivate a growth mind-set while learning to get along with others, right? When you learn to cultivate whole-class discussions in which students can talk about mathematics in a way that reveals their understanding of concepts, critiques their own and others' thinking, and seeks out efficient solutions, your classroom will be completely transformed! These activities will teach your unique and wonderful students to use mathematical discourse effectively.

Mathematical discourse keeps students engaged, focused, and motivated. When students practice mathematical discourse regularly, they learn to link prior knowledge to current understanding. It's really amazing! They learn to make sense of and critique the thinking of others in a respectful way, and these habits become the tools they need to succeed not just in math but in everything they do throughout their whole lives.

Right from the get-go, you must teach children to question each other and explain their reasoning using proper mathematical language. For mathematical discourse to be effective, students and teachers must acknowledge and discuss errors and the reasons behind them in addition to correct answers and strategies. In a discourse-rich classroom, students reach and justify conclusions based on their own mathematical knowledge without relying on teachers. Students are productive and respectful during discourse with proper scaffolds for support. Sound like a lot? It is! It's a whole lot of learning that can be achieved with simple screen-free, hands-on, extremely engaging strategies.

Begin by modeling the discourse. Ask students these questions as they work together to make sense of mathematics:

1. Do you agree?
2. Do you disagree?
3. Can you convince the rest of us that your answer makes sense?
4. What strategy did you use?
5. Would you ask the rest of the class that question?
6. Could you share your method with the class?
7. Did you work together? In what way?
8. Have you discussed this with your group?
9. How could you help someone without telling him or her the answer?
10. Did everybody get a fair chance to talk, use the manipulatives, or be the recorder?

Give students specific questions to guide them in their discourse while they engage in these activities.

Here are important stems and questions that work well:

1. I noticed that _____
2. I can solve this by _____
3. I know that _____
4. I agree because _____
5. I know this because _____
6. I disagree because _____
7. My first step was _____
8. Another strategy you can use is _____
9. How do you know that?
10. What strategy did you use?
11. How did you get your answer?
12. I can prove it by _____

You could write these questions and stems in speech bubbles somewhere in your classroom (even using fluorescent-colored poster board with fancy scalloped edges, if you like!). Another idea is to laminate bookmarks with the twelve questions on them and give one to each child. The children will see these questions posted and have their own to refer to at all times.

Children naturally transfer the enjoyment of literature to math when they learn to see math in their favorite stories. This happens early on when young children see patterns and counting in classic stories like *Goodnight Moon* by Margaret Wise Brown (Harper Festival, 2007) and *Brown Bear, Brown Bear, What Do You See?* by Eric Carle (Henry Holt and Company, 1996). Many children will count out strawberries, apples, and pears after listening to *The Very Hungry Caterpillar* by Eric Carle (Philomel Books, 1994). (This happens for many kids before they can even walk!)

As children get older, they learn the importance of being financially literate with books such as *The Lemonade War* by Jacqueline Davie (HMH Books, 2009) and *Alexander, Who Used to Be Rich Last Sunday* by Judith Viorst (Silver Burdett, 1987). Many kids love the Shel Silverstein poem "Smart" from the anthology *Where the Sidewalk Ends* (HarperCollins, 2014) and can refer to it when making change or trying to figure out how to spend birthday money. Second-grade students could even be inspired to measure the distance from Massachusetts to Pennsylvania when they read *Johnny Appleseed* by Steven Kellogg (HarperCollins, 1998). They could also really enjoy measuring apple orchards (created from card stock) and fences (Lincoln Logs) to "protect" apple trees (play dough creations) from animals (Little People Farm Collection) as part of a STEM challenge.

All teachers know firsthand the power of a good story, so this book connects these opportunities for effective mathematical discourse to books children really love!

ACTIVITY 1: THINK-PAIR-SHARE: LET'S TALK ABOUT JOHNNY APPLESEED

Book and Materials

- *Johnny Appleseed* by Steven Kellogg (HarperCollins, 1998)
- Paper and writing supplies
- Discourse stems and questions

Skills

- Number sense
- Problem solving

The first opportunity for rich mathematical discourse is based on the story of Johnny Appleseed and uses the think-pair-share model.

Kellogg's retelling of the classic tale includes rich and engaging text and beautiful illustrations. The story comes to life in an exciting and heartwarming way. Ask your students why Johnny Appleseed is considered an American hero, and guide them in understanding his love for all humanity.

Think-pair-share is a tried-and-true American pedagogy. Pairing students strategically in order for them to discuss mathematics accomplishes many objectives. It allows students to "rehearse" their responses. Sometimes students don't want to share their ideas in class because they are not sure how to phrase their thoughts. They might not think their ideas are valuable or correct. By first sharing their ideas with a peer, they can sharpen their response if called on to share with the class.

Be sure the discourse stems and questions are accessible as the students work in pairs to solve this problem.

Students will work together to compose groups of ten. It's simple to change the number of buckets and amount of apples needed in each bucket to meet the needs of students at any level.

Johnny Appleseed has ten buckets. He wants to put one apple in each bucket. He already has four apples. How many more apples does he need so there are apples in all ten buckets? The children should work together to draw a picture and write an equation to solve the problem. They will then explain their strategies and solutions to the class.

ACTIVITY 2: THE POWER OF LOW FLOOR/HIGH CEILING TASKS: BARNYARD WALK

Book and Materials

- *Rosie's Walk* by Pat Hutchins (Aladdin, 1971)
- Paper and writing supplies

Skills

- Probability
- Number sense
- Critical thinking

The amazing power of tasks that are low floor/high ceiling (or LFHC, as they are often referred to) is that they are easy to understand and visualize but difficult to solve. They are accessible to students with a wide range of academic abilities and lead to rich mathematical discourse. Children of different ages and levels can work together on the same problem (even if they can't solve it), learn to persevere, and ultimately cultivate a growth mind-set.

Although it seems as if low floor/high ceiling is a new concept in the math realm, it was actually first formulated in the 1970s by Seymour Papert, a professor at MIT who was heavily influenced by Piaget, as a design principle for a programming language called Logo. The idea was to make programming accessible to young children while simultaneously being usable at a more complex level by adults.

This concept allows us the opportunity to provide easy ways for novices to get started (low floor) but also ways for them to work on increasingly sophisticated projects over time (high ceiling). The important thing to remember is that children do not all follow one path from low floor to high ceiling. Teachers need to provide opportunities for discovery so that students can explore multiple pathways from floor to ceiling. The ultimate goal is to help all children develop their thinking, voice, and identity. None of that will happen without providing these opportunities for exploring, experimenting, and expressing themselves.

What makes a low-floor/high-ceiling task special? How do you know if the task you want to use truly fits the criteria and will provide the engagement and exploratory work you hope to accomplish? The following is true about LFHC tasks:

- They require an inquiry approach.
- They do not have a predetermined solution pathway.
- They have many possible representations of solutions and strategies.
- They involve the process of exploring and gaining a deeper understanding of mathematics once the problem is solved.

This LFHC task is based on the book *Rosie's Walk* by Pat Hutchins (Aladdin, 1971). In this simplistic yet wildly humorous story, Rosie the hen takes a walk around the barnyard. But she does not realize a fox is following her. In comical ways, the fox fails in his attempts to catch the hen.

Rosie the hen is trying to climb up a flight of ten steps to escape the fox. She can only hop up one or two steps each time she hops. She never hops down, only up. How many different ways can Rosie hop up the flight of ten steps? Provide evidence to justify your thinking.

There is always awesome, meaningful discussion and so much creativity involved when teachers present this task to students! It's important that students justify their thinking and show their understanding of number sense, counting, and probability.

ACTIVITY 3: SITUATIONAL PROBLEM SOLVING: MILK AND COOKIES FOR EVERYONE!

Book and Materials

- *The Doorbell Rang* by Pat Hutchins (Greenwillow Books, 1989)
- Paper and writing materials

Skills

- Number sense
- Problem solving

Unlike the word problems in many textbooks, situational problems are complex, require some analysis, and have more than one correct answer. They reflect the kind of real-world problem solving people use every day.

This situational problem is based on *The Doorbell Rang* by Pat Hutchins (Greenwillow Books, 1989). Just as a mother serves her children freshly baked cookies, the doorbell rings. As guests enter, the children recalculate the number of cookies for each person to make sure everyone gets the same amount.

Ask students to work with a buddy or in a small group to plan a milk-and-cookies party for some friends. They need to decide how many friends to invite, how much milk they need, and how many cookies they need. Be sure to make the students understand that there is no one correct way to carry out this task. Everyone may have a different idea about how to plan the party, but they need to communicate respectfully and make decisions together. Teachers can provide students with stems for respectful dialogue, such as "I like the idea Jade had because _____ and maybe we can also try _____," or "Although I understand why Brian is suggesting _____, perhaps it might also be effective to try _____." The rich mathematical discourse and evidence of learning will come shining through as students analyze a situation, calculate amounts, and make estimates in an authentic way.

ACTIVITY 4: EXPLORING EQUATIONS AND ORGANIZED THINKING: IT MUST BE ONE HUNDRED!

Book and Materials

- *The Wolf's Chicken Stew* by Keiko Kasza (Puffin Books, 1996)
- Paper and writing supplies

Skills

- Number sense
- Problem solving

The Wolf's Chicken Stew by Keiko Kasza (Puffin Books, 1996) is a perfect connection to this activity. In the story, a hungry wolf wants some chicken stew. He spots a chicken and decides to fatten her up. He feeds her one hundred pancakes, one hundred donuts, and a hundred-pound cake.

In this opportunity for respectful mathematical discourse, students explore equations for one hundred. To present the problem, start by asking students to name different number sentences (equations). Explain that they will explore different equations they can write for one hundred. There is clearly no one right answer to this problem, for the number of possible equations is nearly limitless. What is interesting is how the students tackle the problem, how they organize their thinking, and what kinds of equations they are comfortable listing.

The results can be revealing in a number of ways. Students may begin by randomly listing equations. They may eventually see patterns emerge and decide to start on a fresh piece of paper to organize their equations in some way. Remind them that they need to show and share their thinking, and, as always, have plenty of manipulatives available!

This opportunity can easily be differentiated by changing one hundred to a higher or lower number. Be sure to allow lots of time for a whole-group discussion when this task is complete because the children will be eager and excited to share their strategies and discoveries when challenged in this way. You will definitely want to give all the children a chance to contribute to the discussion.

ACTIVITY 5: SURVEY SAVVY: FAVORITE FRUITS

Book and Materials

- *Eating the Alphabet* by Lois Ehlert (HMH Books for Young Readers, 1996)
- Paper and writing supplies
- Index cards or sticky notes

Skills

- Collecting, organizing, representing, and interpreting data
- Problem solving

In order to understand what statistics mean, students need to start at the beginning, asking a question, recording the answers, showing the answers in an easy-to-grasp form, and seeing what they can learn from this organized information. With this opportunity, students will conduct a survey to find out the class's favorite kind of fruit. First the class as a whole is polled, with students recording the results. Then students are challenged to find a good way to show the data and also tell what they learned from the data.

Eating the Alphabet by Lois Ehlert (HMH Books for Young Readers, 1996) is a beautifully illustrated book and perfect to read before presenting this activity because of the amazing way it introduces fruits and vegetables from all around the world. You will want to spend time exploring the glossary at the end, which provides interesting facts about each food.

To present this mathematical opportunity for effective and engaging discourse, begin as a whole class. Brainstorm different kinds of fruit. Have each child write down on a piece of paper (index cards and sticky notes work well) his or her favorite fruit. Have the children record their votes in secret to prevent them from changing their minds later on.

Next, call on students one at a time to tell what they wrote down. Students can keep track of their classmates' responses any way they choose. Be sure to go slowly enough so everybody can record the responses. You may want to encourage some kind of shorthand way to write the information (A for apple or a quick sketch, for example). When the information is recorded, gather the students' papers and post them, in random order, so students can have access to the data.

Tell students to work together (with a buddy or small group) to find a way to show the information you have all collected so someone from another class could see what your favorite fruits are. Let them know it could be a graph, a chart, a list, or another way they choose.

Finally, have the children explain, as partners or a team, what they can learn from the information they have gathered. They should include pictures, numbers, and words and be able to explain their ideas using proper mathematical language.

Guide the students as they work with these questions:

- What do you want to show?
- How can you show that?
- How can you organize the information you have collected to help you compare people's favorite fruits?
- How can you show that information to make it clear to someone else?
- When you look at your graph/chart/list, what does it tell you?

An important and wonderful thing about this opportunity for mathematical discourse is the way that children take complete ownership of their learning and find creative ways to make the data meaningful. It will be exciting to see and hear the students work together and feel the energy in the room as they display and discuss the authentic data about themselves. Children can and will naturally extend this activity by taking unprompted surveys about other favorite foods and favorite games. You will be amazed when you see your students independently working while learning and having fun!

ACTIVITY 6: PROBLEM FORMULATION: TEDDY BEAR PICNIC

Book and Materials

- *The Teddy Bears' Picnic* by Jimmy Kennedy (Aladdin, 2000)
- Paper and writing supplies

Skills

- Number sense
- Problem solving

This open-ended opportunity for mathematical discourse reverses the students' and teacher's roles. Instead of giving students problems to solve, ask them to come up with their own problems. This role of problem writer puts interesting demands on students. First, they must interpret information from a picture, and then they must try to formulate problems. Students also need to make sure their problems are clearly stated and make sense in the context of the picture. This is an interesting challenge for students of all ages and levels of expertise.

The Teddy Bears' Picnic by Jimmy Kennedy (Aladdin, 2000) is a beautifully illustrated book of the classic teddy bear song. It would be a great choice for this particular activity, but any book or even any illustration will do as long as it has lots of characters, objects, and an interesting topic your students will relate to and enjoy.

To present this opportunity for rich mathematical discourse, make sure your students know what a word problem is. Make up a word problem with them, or show them one they have recently solved in their math journal or textbook, if you use those things. Point out that word problems have numbers and words and end with a question.

Show the children the picture you have chosen or let them choose from a few that are appropriate. Ask the students to make up word problems that can be solved using the picture. You can make it a big deal and be dramatic by saying, "Aren't you *so* tired of solving *other* people's problems? Here is your chance to write your own!"

Tell the students that after they have finished writing up their problems, they should solve them. Next, give them the chance to solve each other's problems. As always, model appropriate mathematical language, and have all discourse stems and questions readily accessible to all students. It will be interesting and exciting to hear the students explain their thinking about why they chose the problems they did and how they solved each other's problems. Of course, this opportunity can be revisited again and again with different books and pictures.

ACTIVITY 7: EXPLORING MEASUREMENT: PUDDLE TROUBLE

Book and Materials

- *Henry and Mudge in Puddle Trouble* by Cynthia Rylant (Simon Spotlight, 1996)
- Paper and writing supplies
- Ruler
- Sponge
- Spoons
- Cubes
- Stick
- Bucket
- Yarn
- Measuring cups
- Drinking cups
- Paper
- Scale

Skills

- Measurement
- Problem solving

This investigation focuses on students' ideas about measurement. It's not a straightforward measurement task like finding the length of a table or a piece of yarn. You will ask your students to measure a puddle, and they will have to decide for themselves just what to measure and what tools to use. It will be fascinating to see the varied and creative methods students come up with to measure a puddle! Some students may use counters to find its area; others might decide to use a sponge to transfer the water to find its volume.

Henry and Mudge in Puddle Trouble by Cynthia Rylant (Simon Spotlight, 1996) is a fun story to set the stage and encourage excitement for this open-ended task. Henry and his 180-pound dog venture out on a wet spring day, and, of course, they are ready for puddle trouble!

Present this problem by starting with this question: What kinds of things would you use to measure a puddle? Display a group of objects that may or may not be helpful in the task, such as the above-listed materials.

These items may encourage the students to think of measuring in a variety of different ways, and it's important for them to have ample time to think and engage in mathematical discourse as they create a plan for measuring a puddle. Have them work together in small groups to show their ideas on paper.

Ask the students these questions to guide them in their plan for measuring and in their discourse:

- What are some different ways you can think of to measure a puddle?
- What will you use to measure the puddle in each different way?
- How can you show all the ways of measuring? Would making sketches help?

This is also a great opportunity for assessment because when you see what tools they use, what they measure, and how many different ways they can come up with, you will see what they have internalized about the work they have done so far in measurement.

ACTIVITY 8: PURPLE, GREEN, AND YELLOW, THEN ADD RED

Book and Materials

- *Purple, Green, and Yellow* by Robert Munsch (Annick, 1992)
- Blocks in at least four different colors
- Paper and crayons or markers

Skills

- Problem solving
- Probability

Robert Munsch is known for his wildly humorous stories about ordinary kids, and *Purple, Green, and Yellow* (Annick, 1992) is definitely a classroom favorite. In the story, Brigid loves using markers. She has all kinds: washable, permanent, and smelly. The trouble begins when she decides to decorate herself but cannot remove the color. Everyone will love the surprise ending in this story that appeals to all ages.

The book is a perfect introduction to this mathematical discourse-rich challenge. Try it with blocks, markers, and paper or with just markers and paper. Ask the children to take three different color blocks—maybe purple, green, and yellow, but any three colors are fine. Have them make a tower using one of each color. Ask them to make and record as many different towers as possible. When they are sure they have found them all, they should try it with a fourth color, maybe red, but of course any color is fine.

It's really important to encourage students, as always, to use the mathematical discourse questions and stems when verbalizing their thinking and critiquing the work of others. You will be amazed to see students' solutions and hear their explanations.

ACTIVITY 9: THE MONEY JAR: SOMETHING SPECIAL TO HELP OTHERS

Book and Materials

- *Something Special for Me* by Vera B. Williams (Greenwillow, 1986)
- Jar or another kind of container
- Play money

Skills

- Financial literacy

This activity will not only give students an opportunity for effective and respectful mathematical discourse as they practice financial literacy skills but also will allow students to take the time to think about what kindness means and focus on doing something special for others.

Something Special for Me by Vera B. Williams (Greenwillow, 1986) is a story about Rosa, Mama, and Grandma. They are a wonderful loving little family who keep a money jar filled with coins that will be emptied to buy Rosa something special for her birthday. When it is finally time to spend the money, Rosa is only happy when she finds something her whole family will enjoy. This message about thinking about others is beautifully delivered and not easily forgotten.

You can create money jars with play coins and give them to small groups of students. Each group has to count the money first and then come up with a plan for spending. The criteria for spending is that they have to spend all the money in the jar on something that will help others. They then show different ways to show the same amount of money.

This is easily adaptable to meet the needs of all students by changing the types and amounts of coins in each jar. This is an activity you can do with young children, using one hundred pennies in a little jar, to have them show all the ways to make a dollar and with much older children with as much as $432 in change. It's a great way to hear their ideas for helping others.

ACTIVITY 10: ON THE LOOKOUT FOR LENGTHS

Book and Materials

- *The Gingerbread Man Loose at the Zoo* by Laura Murray (G. P. Putnam's Sons Books for Young Readers, 2016)
- Measuring tools
- Chart paper and markers

Skills

- Measurement
- Problem solving

When you send students on a scavenger hunt, challenging them to find objects of specific lengths and, of course, reminding them to use respectful, effective mathematical discourse, you will be building community and inspiring authentic learning, and you will also have great anchor charts to display to remind your students about the importance of using measurement benchmarks.

Begin by reading an entertaining book involving a scavenger hunt. Students really enjoy *The Gingerbread Man Loose at the Zoo* by Laura Murray (G. P. Putnam's Sons Books for Young Readers, 2016). It's about a gingerbread man who is on a field trip to the zoo but gets lost and has to use clues to find his way back to his classmates. He ends up on a wild scavenger hunt where he meets giraffes, monkeys, and even a fox!

To begin your own scavenger hunt and send students off searching for lengths in an organized way, place the children in groups. Give each group a different length. Ask each student to find an appropriate measuring tool, and send each one off in search of objects of his or her designated length. After a specified time, have each student group meet and respectfully discuss their findings. They decide together which objects meet the criteria. A lot of times students will bring the same types of objects and then go back and search together so they will have a variety to work with.

It will be interesting to hear how students guide each other, urging their peers to look at different angles and sides of objects to find things to add to their collections. Once the groups have all had a chance to search and are happy with the results, provide materials for each group to create a poster illustrating the objects they found. Display the posters in the classroom to serve as measurement benchmarks and reminders of their collaborative work.

ACTIVITY 11: NEW CLOTHES FOR THE PRINCIPAL, PLEASE!

Book and Materials

- *The Principal's New Clothes* by Stephanie Calmenson (Scholastic, 1989)
- A photocopied picture of the principal for each small group of students
- Paper and writing supplies
- Crayons

Skills

- Problem solving
- Logical thinking
- Patterns and relationships

Tell the students that there is an emergency situation—the principal needs new clothes. Read *The Principal's New Clothes* by Stephanie Calmenson (Scholastic, 1989) to create more enthusiasm about this dilemma. Make a photocopy of a picture of the principal for each group of children. Give them another piece of paper to create three tops and two pairs of pants. Ask them to figure out how many different outfits the principal would be able to make with the pieces of clothing they created. Tell them that the principal doesn't ever want to repeat an outfit and to keep creating outfits until everyone in the group is sure that there are no more possible combinations.

The study of patterns and relationships, problem-solving strategies, and logical thinking can easily be made more challenging by changing the number of clothing pieces and criteria for what is considered an appropriate outfit. It will be fun to see the reaction when you show the actual principal the outfits created for him or her.

ACTIVITY 12: PEANUTS, PLEASE!

Book and Materials

- *Take Me Out to the Ballgame* by Jack Norworth (Aladdin, 1999)
- One cup of peanuts or popcorn per small group of students
- Blank paper
- Pencils
- Scissors
- Tape
- Rulers
- Stapler

Skills

- Describing and measuring geometric shapes
- Estimation
- Using spatial sense
- Problem solving

In this investigation, students tackle a packaging problem and in the process explore different ways they can put shapes together to form three-dimensional containers with the capacity of one cup. A lot of authentic planning and measuring goes into this task, and some trial and error, resulting in inventive ways for solving this problem.

This is a great opportunity for students to use mathematical discourse as they describe and measure geometric shapes, think visually, use spatial sense, and estimate.

Read *Take Me Out to the Ballgame* by Jack Norworth (Aladdin, 1999). Tell the students to pretend we are all going to a special ballgame and need to create our own peanut (or popcorn if your class has peanut allergies) containers. We are allowed to bring one cup of peanuts each and cannot take plastic bags out to the stadium. Show them a bag with exactly one measured cup of peanuts in it.

Tell the students that their job is to make a container that will hold one cup of peanuts. Set up a station with the construction materials listed above. Have them first create a plan and then by trial and error improve on their design until they are happy with the final result. They should record their ideas and results as they work.

Guide them with these questions as they work:

- What different shapes could your container be?
- How will you know what size to make your container?
- If your container is not the right size, how could you change it so it holds just one cup?

Once they have made a container shape they like, they should test it by filling it with a cup of peanuts. For the testing phase, set up a center with a tub of peanuts and measuring cups.

When the students are happy with their container designs, have them finish their reports and present them. The reports should contain their initial plan, their trial-and-error attempts, and a sketch of the container with measurements. When the students are presenting, it's important to remind everyone to explain their ideas carefully and to be active, respectful listeners.

ACTIVITY 13: STURDY SHAPES

Book and Materials

- *The Three Little Pigs* by Paul Galdone (HMH Books, 1984)
- Toothpicks
- Miniature marshmallows or clay
- Pictures of structures that have been built with triangular supports, such as pyramids, bridges, and girders

Skills

- Creating and comparing three-dimensional shapes
- Problem solving

Read the classic version of the *Three Little Pigs* by Paul Galdone (HMH Books, 1984) to your class. Because this fairy tale has been rewritten so many times and in such creative ways, it's easy to find other versions to suit any age group, but start with the classic for this activity. Encourage children to talk about the building materials used by each pig in the story. Discuss why the brick house was sturdier than houses built of straw or sticks.

In this activity the students will use geometry to find a sturdy shape. Tell them they are going to work with a buddy to try to make a house that's "wolf-proof" and won't easily collapse. Before presenting this activity to the class, make a triangle and square out of toothpicks and marshmallows. Recall with the class the reason the wolf was able to blow down the house of straw and house of sticks. Explain to the children that just as some building materials make stronger houses than others, some shapes are "stronger" than others. Hold up the toothpick triangle and rectangle, and ask the children to say which they think is stronger. Be sure they explain their answers using the mathematical discourse stems.

Divide the class in pairs. Assign one child in each pair to make the triangle and the other to make the square. Distribute miniature marshmallows (or balls of clay) and toothpicks, and if necessary model how to make each shape.

When the shapes are completed, show children how to push gently on the top of each shape. What happens? As children see that the square collapses more easily, have them explain why they think this is happening. What conclusions can they come up with about which shape is stronger?

Show students pictures of structures that have been built using triangular shapes at this point in the lesson (e.g., the pyramids, bridges that have triangular supports, girders that form building supports). If you can, have an engineer, contractor, architect, or other building professional visit to talk to your class about geometry. Ask the speaker to emphasize concepts such as the strength of different materials and shapes in language appropriate for whatever level you are teaching.

It's rewarding to take the time to plan and combine important mathematical concepts and discourse with classic literature and relevant social studies topics. When you do this, you create an environment where the children are given time to focus, think, and contemplate, and you inspire the authentic learning you really and truly want to happen.

Let's Talk about Math!

ACTIVITY 14: BUGS, BUGS, BUGS

Books and Materials

- *The Very Busy Spider* by Eric Carle (Philomel Books, 1983)
- *The Very Lonely Firefly* by Eric Carle (Philomel Books, 1999)
- Paper and pencils

Skills

- Number sense
- Problem solving

The Very Busy Spider (Philomel Books, 1983) and *The Very Lonely Firefly* (Philomel Books, 1999) by Eric Carle are classic, beautiful stories providing children with knowledge about spiders and insects and also delivering messages about cooperation and belonging.

Be sure the discourse stems and questions are accessible as the students work together to solve this problem. If your students are not able to add numbers one to sixty-eight, or if they are not challenged enough working within one to sixty-eight, change the numbers of insects and legs to meet their needs.

A spider has eight legs, and a firefly has six legs. There are eight spiders and fireflies all together. There are sixty-eight legs in all. Find the number of spiders and the number of fireflies.

The children should work together to draw a picture and write an equation to solve the problem. They will then explain their strategies and solutions to the class. This problem is a great opportunity for students to share strategies and discover new ways to explore and make conjectures. It's important to recognize that students will make mistakes because of this. As all educators know, it's important to remind students constantly that errors are expected and natural and that they are a good thing because they lead to enhanced learning.

ACTIVITY 15: WILL THE BOAT STILL FLOAT?

Book and Materials

- *Who Sank the Boat?* by Pamela Allen (Puffin Books, 1996)
- Access to a sink or tub and water
- Aluminum foil
- Various objects such as plastic cubes, marbles, erasers, and paper clips

Skills

- Measuring by weight
- Estimation
- Problem solving

Skills including the process of measuring by weight, estimation, and the reasonableness of answers, as well as actual measurement of weight, are practiced with this last but certainly not least literature-based opportunity for mathematical discourse.

Start by reading the book *Who Sank the Boat?* by Pamela Allen (Puffin Books, 1996). In this story five animal friends go for a ride in a rowboat. As each gets in, the added weight causes the boat to tip precariously. Children love guessing which animal will sink the boat and are pleasantly surprised by the ending.

Be sure the discourse stems and questions are accessible as the students work together to design aluminum foil boats, estimate the weight they can carry, and check their answers by weighing and adding items. This activity can be adapted by keeping boats small and limiting the weight each will carry.

Cooperative groups will fill a sink or tub almost half full of water. They will then use foil to make a boat and try floating their boat on the water. They will estimate how much weight it will carry and still float. Students will then weigh various objects, such as plastic cubes, erasers, paper clips, and marbles. They will add them to the boat, recording the weight they are adding so they will know when they have reached their estimated weight.

The children should work together to find out how much weight their boat will carry, and each group member should be able to explain to the class the group's strategies, process, any problems that occurred, how they overcame them, and the solution. When meeting with a whole group after students have worked in groups of three or four, you may choose to assign each student in the group a number. For example, when number 3 is called, all students who are given number 3 should respond. Students will then know that any member of the group may be called on to provide a response, so everyone needs to have the same level of understanding.

Students will not all naturally have conversations in which they reveal their understanding of concepts, critique their own and others' ideas, and seek out efficient mathematical solutions. Some might. The overwhelming majority of students will not. However, the modeling, the prompts, and the commitment to hold students accountable for both listening and speaking is all it takes to give students the power to persevere and succeed.

It takes courage to mix things up and conviction to push yourself to the limit. Teachers may not always feel they have what it takes to be the teacher they want to be. However, when they do push themselves to the limit, and even beyond that limit, the reward is meaningful moments that exude passion, creativity, and authenticity. Teachers owe it to themselves and to their students to be the dynamic, influential educators they know they were truly meant to be.

Success is the sum of small efforts, repeated day in and day out.
—Robert Collier

Chapter Four

Collaborative and Meaningful Literacy Centers

Fifteen Opportunities for Students to Extend Their Learning in Creative and Challenging Ways

Literacy is a journey, not a race.

—Bonnie Hill Campbell

Students of all ages love the challenge and freedom that working in literacy centers promotes. Literacy centers allow students to interact with peers, explore, be creative, and apply newly learned concepts and skills in meaningful ways. Teachers can design instruction and practice for a variety of literacy skills while creating a risk-free, positive atmosphere for learning when they take the time to implement meaningful literacy centers.

The literacy centers in this chapter will provide important work for students and also give them opportunities to collaborate, create, use critical-thinking skills, and communicate. Students should treat each center as a valuable learning experience and not as free time. Every classroom should have clear rules and expectations established to be sure students are both successful and comfortable when working in centers. Here are some suggested literacy center rules:

- Use a quiet "inside" voice.
- Share materials.
- Take only the materials you need and clean up.
- Work hard the entire time.
- When the teacher is working with small groups, do not interrupt.

- Be kind and respectful.
- Use accountable talk.

Accountable talk should be taught and reinforced throughout every part of the school day, especially at center time when collaboration is a must. Students find it helpful to have accountable talk prompts to refer to when working on their own within collaborative groups at literacy centers. Teachers can write them on an anchor chart, give them to students on printed bookmarks, or create brightly colored speech bubbles with the prompts written inside to hang around the room. Here are some suggested accountable talk prompts:

- I was wondering _____
- Could you explain _____
- When you said _____ I didn't understand _____
- Can you explain what you mean in a different way?
- Also, I think _____
- Have you thought about _____?
- I agree/disagree because _____
- I like what you said about _____

Once rules and expectations are made clear, and students are reminded to use appropriate accountable talk while working in the literacy centers, teachers often spend several days training students to work at the centers and making sure they are following the proper procedures. The ultimate goal is for students to work independently in their collaborative groups while the teacher is instructing other small groups.

It will often take time to introduce each center, explain where to get materials, and role-play using a "whisper voice." When taught and given time to practice, students can read, play games, complete group tasks, and communicate effectively without disturbing the teacher. Many teachers find it useful to have a hand signal or bell to use in case the noise level gets too high. Wireless doorbells are a fun option, and there are many models available with multiple sound choices.

Take the time to observe students and reinforce the literacy center rules and expectations; this will enable students to be successful and comfortable as they take control of their own learning and have fun working and collaborating. Students will learn time-management, interpersonal, and decision-making skills as well as strengthen their literacy skill knowledge.

Each center in this chapter has a theme with a variety of activities that can be easily adapted to meet the needs of students at any grade or level. It's important for teachers to regularly watch the centers in action to determine which seem most effective and engaging and which need fine-tuning.

LITERACY CENTER 1: POETRY CENTER

Objective

Students will explore poetry in a variety of ways. They will apply a wide range of reading strategies, such as connecting background knowledge, creating visual imagery, making predictions, inferring, and asking questions. Students will grow as critical thinkers as they discuss authors' purposes for writing, explore their feelings, and make personal connections to texts.

Materials

- Poetry books
- Writing materials
- Magnetic words/board or commercially produced magnetic poetry kit

Activities

- Students can work together to choose a poem and set it to a familiar tune. They might also record it or perform it for the class at a designated time.
- Students can use premade word tiles to create their own poems on a magnetic board or even a cookie sheet. The poems can also be written and compiled into a class book of original poems, or they can be photographed, printed, and hung in the center to inspire others.
- Students can select a poem and create illustrations to go with it. The collaborative group might choose to create their own individual pictures to go with one poem or work together to make one picture as a group.
- Students can work together to memorize and dramatize a poem and later perform it for the class.
- Students can choose a poem and think about the main idea. They can discuss as a group and then work together to continue the idea to add a new verse to the poem.
- Students can work together to create an ongoing list of similes and metaphors in poetry. They can record their findings on a class chart or in a notebook.
- Students can use a T-chart or other graphic organizer to compare two similar poems. They can be assigned two poems or decide as a group on a particular topic, choose two poems that are related to it, and list similarities and differences.
- Students can create fill-in-the-blank poems. A poem can be selected and written out but with adjectives and other parts of speech missing. The kids can fill in the missing words and make their own humorous poems.

Suggested Literature

- *Where the Sidewalk Ends* by Shel Silverstein (HarperCollins, 2014)
- *A Light in the Attic* by Shel Silverstein (HarperCollins, 2009)
- *No More Homework! No More Tests!: Kids' Favorite Funny School Poems* by Bruce Lansky (Running Press Adult, 1997)
- *Honey, I Love and Other Poems* (Reading Rainbow Series) by Eloise Greenfield (HarperCollins, 1986)
- *Tomie dePaola's Mother Goose* by Tomie dePaola (G. P. Putnam's Sons for Young Readers, 1985)
- *The 20th Century Children's Poetry Treasury* by Jack Prelutsky (Knopf Books for Young Readers, 1999)

LITERACY CENTER 2: FAMOUS PEOPLE CENTER

Objective

Students will read and explore a variety of sources for the purpose of researching and learning about other people. They will reflect on their reading and respond in meaningful ways.

Materials

- A variety of biographies that accommodate the range of reading levels in the classroom
- Photos of famous people
- Paper and writing supplies
- Markers or crayons

Activities

- Students can work together to research a famous person and write a news story as if they were reporters covering an event for which the person is famous. They must include who, what, when, where, why, and how in their story and create at least one picture that might have been taken during the event.
- Students can imagine they traveled back in time to spend a week with the person they choose to research. They can write about their time with the person, making sure to include factual information they have found through research.
- Students can work together to create a time line for a certain person's life. The group can research a person they choose together and decide what the

important parts of that person's life are and how they can best display them in a chronological way.
- Students can work as a group to select a famous event in history. They should research the people involved in the event and the role each one played. They can then dramatize the event, being sure to accurately portray the people and details according to their research.
- Students can explore character traits and use text evidence in a collaborative way with this activity. They should choose a famous person to research, decide on three to five character traits that best describe the person, and document the evidence in the text to support each trait. They can do this in individual journals or in one group report.
- Students can work together to make a "collectible" trading card about a person they decide to research. They need to find out the most important information about the person and decide how to present it in a concise, accurate way on an index card or paper cut into fourths. One side of the card can show a picture of the person, and the other side can have the information. Students might also decide to create a group of trading cards with a common theme. For example, they can choose three to five different presidents, athletes, or authors, and each member of the group can create one card with the group of cards displayed together.
- Students can work together to explore and discuss conflict and solution by researching a given or chosen person and deciding what conflicts or major struggles the person overcame. They can record the conflicts and solutions in personal notebooks or in one group report and present their findings to the class at a later scheduled date and time.
- Students can work together to reflect on a given or chosen quote from a famous person. They can discuss what they think the quote means and how it can be applied to their own lives. Students can create a visual interpretation with pictures or write their ideas in a cooperative narrative writing piece.

Suggested Literature

- *National Geographic Little Kids First Big Book of Who* (National Geographic Little Kids First Big Books) by Jill Esbaum (National Geographic Children's Books, 2015)
- *Who Was Walt Disney?* (Who Was?) by Whitney Stewart (Penguin, 2009)
- *Who Was Albert Einstein?* (Who Was?) by Jess Brallier (Penguin, 2002)
- *Rising Above: How 11 Athletes Overcame Challenges in Their Youth to Become Stars* by Gregory Zuckerman (Puffin Books, 2017)
- *The Big Book of Presidents: From George Washington to Barack Obama* by Nancy J. Hajeski (Sky Pony, 2015)

- *Women in Science: 50 Fearless Pioneers Who Changed the World* by Rachel Ignotofsky (Ten Speed Press, 2016)

LITERACY CENTER 3: GEOGRAPHY CENTER

Objective

Students will read and respond to a variety of sources to gain knowledge about the world. Students will apply literacy skills at their own level of expertise to learn about continents, countries, regions, states, and landforms.

Materials

- Books (fiction and nonfiction) that represent specific locations
- Maps
- Postcards
- Travel brochures
- Flags
- Plastic animals, props, spices, clothing, and other items that represent a specific location
- Paper and writing supplies
- Markers or crayons
- Bulletin board and pushpins

Activities

- Students can make group landform books in which they explain and represent major types of landforms. They will need to include a page for these landforms: volcano, valley, river, plain, ocean, mountain, lake, island, hill, desert, canyon. Students can use a dictionary to look up the definitions and various resources provided in the center for other details. The books can then be kept in the geography center. As the students learn about different areas, they can add the area to their book on the appropriate landform page.
- Students can create region posters. Each small group can choose one region or landform of the United States, such as mountains, deserts, the Great Lakes, and so on. They need to research their chosen topics and then create a poster with accurate information. They should work together to draw different features of the area, labeling it with the name of the region or landform and writing a short passage about it.
- Once students have explored several kinds of maps, they can create a map of their classroom, school, or an imaginary location. They should make

symbols to show important features of their place and create a key, with symbols defined, for their map.
- Students can work together to write directions for getting from place to place based on maps from different places, such as malls, parks, and their own city and state.
- After students have experience with reading travel brochures and understand their purpose and content, they can design and create their own based on a place they have researched or are learning about.
- Students can sort maps according to their type and discuss similarities and differences among them.
- Students can work together to create a book about an assigned or chosen location. They should work together in their group to research, choose the information they want to present, and decide how they want to design their book. The books can be kept permanently in the geography center or classroom library.
- Students can write to different states and/or countries to request materials for the geography center.

Suggested Literature

- *Me on the Map* (Rise and Shine) by National Geographic Learning (National Geographic School Publications, 2003)
- *National Geographic Kids World Atlas*, Fifth Edition by National Geographic Kids (National Geographic Children's Books, 2018)
- *Maps of the World: An Illustrated Children's Atlas of Adventure, Culture, and Discovery* by Enrico Lavagno (Black Dog and Leventhal, 2018)
- *Where on Earth?: The Ultimate Atlas of What's Where in the World* by DK (DK Children, 2013)
- *The Everything Kids' Geography Book: From the Grand Canyon to the Great Barrier Reef—Explore the World!* by Jane P. Gardner (Adams, 2009)
- *Maps and Globes* by Jack Knowlton (Collins, 1986)

LITERACY CENTER 4: POST OFFICE/MESSAGE CENTER

Objective

Students will write for a variety of purposes and in various forms, applying level-appropriate skills taught in formal writing groups and lessons, to communicate with others.

Materials

- Paper
- Envelopes
- Writing and art supplies
- Bulletin board or other type of message board
- Pushpins
- Sticky notes
- Stamps
- Letter-writing resources
- *The Celebrity Black Book 2015: Over 50,000 Celebrity Addresses* by contactanycelebrity.com (Mega Niche Media, 2015)
- Fairy-tale anthology such as *The Golden Book of Fairy Tales* (Golden Classics) by Adrienne Segur (Golden Books, 1999)
- Names and room numbers of other teachers and students in the building
- Bins for outgoing/incoming mail

Activities

- Teachers can choose a few celebrities from a book with real addresses, such as the above mentioned by contactanycelebrity.com, or let students have access to the book and decide as a group who they would like to write to.
- Students can respond to an open-ended question from the teacher or another adult in the building. Students should be given guidelines such as how long the response should be and whether each member of the group should do his or her own writing or if it is acceptable for one student to write down the group's ideas.
- Students can follow a secret code or work as a team to develop their own to send messages to teachers and other students. They can also decide to do this only within their small group, creating the code together and writing to each other when they visit the center.
- Students can write a letter to a fairy-tale character. Each member of the team can write a letter to a different character from the same fairy tale or they can work together to write one group letter to any chosen character.
- Students can work together to choose a favorite author and write letters to him or her about different books they enjoyed. Each group member can write about a different book, and the letters can all be mailed together.
- Students can add messages to an ongoing message board. Messages can be written on sticky notes or regular scraps of paper and should be positive, decided on as a team, and meaningful to all.

- Students can work together to write a letter to the cafeteria staff or custodians, showing their appreciation by stating specific things the staff members have done that students are thankful for.
- Students can work together to create a book that compiles letters to the students' families about everything they do and learn about throughout the day. Once each group writes a letter together, the letters can be put together into a book and sent home for families to read on a rotating basis. The book can be updated throughout the year as students learn more and more and have more to write about.

Suggested Literature

- *The Post Office Book: Mail and How It Moves* by Gail Gibbons (Collins, 1986)
- *Dear Mr. Blueberry* by Simon James (Aladdin, 1996)
- *A Letter to Amy* by Ezra Jack Keats (Puffin, 1998)
- *Dear Juno* by Soyung Pak (Puffin Books, 2001)
- *Don't Forget to Write* by Martina Selway (Ideal's Children's Books, 1992)
- *Dear Mr. Henshaw* by Beverly Cleary (HarperCollins, 2000)

LITERACY CENTER 5: OUTSIDE THE WINDOW CENTER

Objective

Students will have opportunities to practice literacy skills at their own level of expertise while exploring the weather, nature, and environment outside their classroom windows.

Materials

- Access to a window
- Paper
- Writing and art supplies
- Cloud guide or book with cloud names and descriptions, such as *The Cloud Book* by Tomie dePaola (Holiday House, 1975)
- Thermometer
- Bird feeder in view of window
- Bird guide or book with bird names and descriptions such as *National Geographic Backyard Guide to the Birds of North America* by Jonathan Alderfer (National Geographic, 2011)
- Graph paper

Activities

- Students can illustrate and describe the clouds they see. They can work together to accurately represent them in a log or in individual reports. Students may also work as a team to research the names of the cloud types they notice and record observations of connections between clouds and weather.
- Students can check the temperature outside and create a graph to study trends in temperatures over a week or even a month. They can work together as a team to come up with words to describe the temperature, create formal weather reports, and even read the reports to the class, pretending to have their own weather show.
- Students can create ongoing season logs by recording evidence of each season in one designated spot. It could be a journal for each team, individual reports they work on together to complete, or an anchor chart divided into four seasonal parts. Students can add information about leaf color, plants, clothing, temperature, animals, and precipitation throughout the year as they visit the center.
- Students can study birds that live near their school if a bird feeder is hung in view of the classroom windows. They can write descriptions of the birds they see and research to find out names and more information about each bird type.
- Students can look for shapes and patterns outside their window. They can work together to keep track of the various shapes they see in nature, in the sky, and in buildings and other structures they notice. They can record their findings in journals or group reports to present to the whole class at a later date.
- Students can work together to create an alphabet book about all the things they see outside their windows. Each cooperative group can work on a selected group of letters and then bind the pages into a book to keep in the center or classroom library.
- Students can work together to write a haiku poem about the area they see outside their windows. The haiku structure has three lines, totaling seventeen syllables. The first line has five syllables, the second has seven, and the third line has five syllables like the first. Punctuation and capitalization are optional.
- Students can work together to come up with an improvement for the area outside their windows. They can draw and write about something they feel would make the area better, stating exactly what would need to happen and why it would be beneficial. For example, students might want to create a vegetable garden to have healthy snacks or put up a tent for shade to play under.

Suggested Literature

- *The Reasons for Seasons* by Gail Gibbons (Holiday House, 1995)
- *Watching the Seasons* (Welcome Books: Watching Nature) by Edana Eckart (Children's Press, 2004)
- *The Kids' Book of Weather Forecasting* (Kids Can!) by Mark Breen (Ideals, 2008)
- *Oh Say Can You Say What's the Weather Today? All about Weather* (Cat in the Hat's Learning Library) by Tish Rabe (Random House Books for Young Readers, 2004)
- *A Backyard Birding Adventure: What's in Your Yard?* by Kermit Cummings (Brown Books Kids, 2015)
- *Backyard Bugs: An Identification Guide to Common Insects, Spiders, and More* by Jaret C. Daniels (Adventure, 2017)

LITERACY CENTER 6: RESPONDING BY CONSTRUCTING

Objective

Students will read and respond to literature that is based on machines and inventions. They will apply level-appropriate literacy skills as they collaborate and create meaningful, inventive, book-based projects. The center activities listed require three specific books but can be easily adapted to connect with any books that have machines or inventions as a main focus.

Materials

- *Stay Away from the Junkyard!* by Tricia Tusa (Simon and Schuster Children's Publishing, 1988)
- Paper
- Writing supplies
- Art supplies
- Large chart or butcher paper
- Recyclable items such as empty food boxes, egg cartons, scraps of wood, cardboard, yarn, and Styrofoam packing
- Scissors
- Tape and glue
- *The Caboose Who Got Loose* by Bill Peet (HMH Books for Young Readers, 2008)
- Train set
- Construction paper and craft materials such as popsicle sticks, play dough, and boxes

- *The Mouse and the Motorcycle* by Beverly Cleary (HarperCollins, 2016)
- Modeling clay and plastic knives for sculpting

Activities

- Students can read or listen to a recording of *Stay Away from the Junkyard* by Tricia Tusa and then write a report describing Mr. Crampton's junk sculpture at the end of the book. Students can discuss how the sculpture makes them feel, what it reminds them of, and whether or not they have ever seen anything quite like it. They will gather their thoughts as a group and decide how they are going to present their ideas in a team report.
- Students will create their own sculpture based on Mr. Crampton's junk sculpture in the above-mentioned book by Tricia Tusa. They can work as a

team to decide what recyclable materials they will use, what steps they need to follow to put them together, and how they want their sculpture to look. They will write about their design process and provide clear, detailed, step-by-step directions that will allow someone else to replicate their sculpture.
- Students can write the story of *Stay Away from the Junkyard* by Tricia Tusa from a different perspective. They need to brainstorm to decide what Clarissa Pig would say if she was describing the adventure of Theo visiting Otis Crampton. Each cooperative group that visits the center should create a story with text and illustrations that they will share with the class at a later time.
- Students can read or listen to a recording of *The Caboose Who Got Loose* by Bill Peet and then extend the story by writing about what they think will happen next. Groups should be encouraged to be creative in both their writing and illustrating and should be given time to share their original story endings with the class.
- Students will enjoy putting together a real train set and creating props to enhance the set after reading or listening to the above story by Bill Peet. Cooperative groups can work together to assemble the set and then create labels and signs for the cars of the train. They can also make tunnels, trees, and cutouts of people with various recyclable items and craft supplies. It's important for students to be encouraged to be creative as they collaborate and that they have time to share their group experience with the whole class.
- Students can read or listen to *The Mouse and the Motorcycle* by Beverly Cleary and create their own model of a motorcycle using modeling clay and a plastic knife. There is a section in chapter 2 that describes how the motorcycle looked to Ralph, the mouse. Teachers can assign this part for students to read or have it recorded for students to listen to. After students create their own original motorcycles, they can write their own description as if they were Ralph the mouse looking at it and speaking.
- Students can create their own story about having Ralph in the classroom. They can use character traits they notice in Ralph and their own imaginations to write one collaborative story or an entire chapter book, with students each contributing their own chapter for a team novel. Stories and novels can be placed in the classroom library for all to enjoy.
- Students can make a mural, illustrating and labeling the main events in the story. The groups can work together to decide what the most important events are and how they are going to present them in their mural. They can use large chart paper or construction paper attached with tape and then display it in the machine and invention center.

Literature Suggestions

- *Crafting with Recyclables* (How-to Library) by Dana Meachen Rau (Cherry Lake, 2013)
- *Recyclables* (Make It With . . .) by Anna Llimaos Plomer (Book House, 2017)
- *DK Eyewitness Books: Train: Discover the Story of Railroads from the Age of Steam to the High-Speed Trains of Today* by John Coiley (DK Children, 2009)
- *Steam, Smoke, and Steel: Back in Time with Trains* by Patrick O'Brien (Charlesbridge, 2000)
- *Motorcycles for Kids: A Children's Picture Book about Motorcycles: A Great Simple Picture Book for Kids to Learn about Different Types of Motorcycles* by Melissa Ackerman (CreateSpace, 2016)
- *Motorcycles!* (Step into Reading) by Susan E. Goodman (Random House Books, 2007)

LITERACY CENTER 7: WRITING ABOUT FEELINGS CENTER

Objective

Students will write and share stories about their feelings, applying their grade-level knowledge of grammar and usage.

Materials

- Paper (a variety of choices)
- Writing supplies
- Blank books
- Comic book templates

Activities

The following writing prompts can be presented at the center as assignments or choices. Students should be given the opportunity to write on different types of paper, in a blank book, or on a comic book template. Teachers should manage the time so that students are writing individual stories for part of the time at the center and sharing their work with the small group for another part of the time.

- Write about a time you were surprised.
- How do you feel when you wake up and it's a snow day?
- Write about how you think you would feel if you saw a friend get hurt.

- Pretend you just won a huge prize. How do you think you would feel?
- Make a list of things that make you laugh. Write about your favorite thing on your list.
- What makes you sad? Why does this make you sad?
- How would you feel if no one wanted to play with you?
- How do you feel when your teacher gives you a special job?

Literature Suggestions

- *The Way I Feel* by Janan Cain (Parenting Press, 2000)
- *What Should Danny Do?* (The Power to Choose) by Adir Levy (Elon Books, 2017)
- *Even Superheroes Have Bad Days* by Shelly Becker (Sterling Children's Books, 2016)
- *Be Kind* by Pat Zietlow Miller (Roaring Brook Press, 2018)
- *Visiting Feelings* by Lauren Rubenstein (Magination Press, 2013)
- *Alexander and the Terrible, Horrible, No Good, Very Bad Day* by Judith Viorst (Atheneum Books for Young Readers, 1972)

LITERACY CENTER 8: MYSTERY WRITING CENTER

Objective

Students will write and share mystery stories, applying their grade-level knowledge of grammar and usage.

Materials

- Paper (a variety of choices)
- Writing supplies
- Blank books
- Props such as detective caps, glasses, magnifying glasses

Activities

The following mystery story prompts can be presented to the students in the center as assignments or choices. Students should be given the opportunity to use a variety of different paper and writing supplies and also use props to pretend to be detectives while they are writing their stories. Time in the center should be managed so students spend time writing individual stories and then sharing the stories within their small group.

- A boy looked in the mirror and saw that his face was ____. He doesn't know why.
- You find a note in your library book. It is written in code.
- Every day a different lunch box disappears at school.
- Your dog dug up a strange bone at the beach.
- All of a sudden the light goes on in the attic, but there's nobody there.
- All the spoons go missing from your house.
- A strange spaceship landed on the playground at school.
- There is a note in the pocket of your jacket. It says, "Be careful of the ____."

Literature Suggestions

- Magic Tree House Series by Mary Pope Osborne (Random House Books for Young Readers, 2001)
- Encyclopedia Brown Series by Donald J. Sobol (Puffin Books, 2007)
- Rebekah—Girl Detective Books 1–8: Fun Short Story Mysteries for Children Ages 9–12 by P. J. Ryan (Magic Umbrella, 2013)
- *Ada Lace, on the Case* by Emily Calandrelli (Simon and Schuster Books for Young Readers, 2017)
- The Boxcar Children Series by Gertrude Chandler Warner (Albert Whitman and Company, 1990)
- Nancy Drew Mystery Series by Carolyn Keene (Grosset and Dunlap, 2015)

LITERACY CENTER 9: JOKE WRITING CENTER

Objective

Students will write and share jokes, applying their grade-level knowledge of grammar and usage.

Materials

- Paper (a variety of choices)
- Writing supplies
- Blank books
- Comic strip templates
- Joke books (see suggested literature)
- Props such as silly glasses, clown noses, and other fun and comical accessories

Activities

Students can use the listed topics and suggested literature as inspiration to write their own jokes. They should have the opportunity to choose from different types of paper and writing supplies and be encouraged to use comical props to make their joke writing and sharing even more entertaining. Students should manage their time in the center so that they have time to write several jokes and also share them with the other students in the cooperative work group.

- Write a joke about an animal that lives in the jungle. What can it do? What does it look like?
- Write a joke about an ice-cream truck. How fast does it travel? Where does it stop?
- Write a joke about a frog. Who are his friends? What does he eat?
- Write a joke about a race car. Where does it race? Who drives it?
- Write a joke about a birthday cake. How large is it? What's inside it?
- Write a joke about a farm. Who lives on it? What kinds of work have to be done?
- Write a joke about a family. How many people are in it? What do they do for fun?
- Write a joke about a zoo. Who takes care of it? Who visits it?

Literature Suggestions

- *Jokes for Kids: The Best Jokes, Riddles, Tongue Twisters, Knock-Knock Jokes, and One-liners for Kids* by Rob Stevens (CreateSpace, 2018)
- *Laugh-Out-Loud Jokes for Kids* by Rob Elliott (Revell, 2010)
- *Ridiculous Riddles* by National Geographic Kids (National Geographic Children's Books, 2012)
- *Knock Knock! The Biggest, Best Joke Book Ever* (Highlights Laugh Attack! Joke Books) by Highlights (Highlights Press, 2017)
- *Seriously Silly Jokes for Kids: Joke Book for Boys and Girls Ages 7–12* (Volume 1) by Wally Brown (CreateSpace, 2018)
- *Best Joke Book for Kids: Best Funny Jokes and Knock-Knock Jokes (200+ Jokes)* by Peter MacDonald (CreateSpace, 2013)

LITERACY CENTER 10: EXPLORING CAREERS CENTER

Objective

Students will have opportunities to discover and explore different careers as they engage in a variety of activities that integrate reading and writing.

Materials

- Paper
- Writing supplies
- Chart paper or poster board
- Art supplies such as paint, paintbrushes, markers, colored pencils, and construction paper
- Play dough or clay
- Recyclable items such as boxes, empty food containers, and Styrofoam
- Various books about different careers (see suggested literature and specific titles for each activity)

Activities

- Students can research different careers and choose one to report about as a team. They should include the education and skills required and describe the type of work that is done in each career. Students ages eight and up will find the book *100 Things to Be When You Grow Up* by Lisa M. Gerry (National Geographic Children's Books, 2017) helpful. The book *When I Grow Up* by Tim Minchin (Scholastic, 2018) is more appropriate for younger students. They can present their findings on a poster board or as a book and share it with the whole class at a later assigned time.
- Students can pretend to be a graphic arts designer and create a cereal box. They can work together as a team to come up with a logo, words to describe the cereal, and an entertaining gimmick or prize that might come with the cereal. Provide empty boxes for them to cover with paper and design, and allow the groups to share their original cereal boxes with the whole class.
- Students can pretend to be fashion designers and design costumes for a new movie. They can decide together as a group what the movie will be about; who the characters will be; and the colors, patterns, and materials the costumes would require. They should write down their ideas for the movie and characters and actually create representations of the costumes in a paper-doll style, using arts and crafts supplies for embellishments and details. Teachers should set aside a time for students to share their ideas and costume representations with the whole class.
- Students can pretend to be pastry chefs and design a wedding cake or other celebratory cake for a special couple or event. They need to work together as a team to decide and write about the people, the event, and all the details about the cake. Students can then create a play dough version or painting representation of the cake to present to the class along with their details about the event and couple.

- Students can imagine what it's like to be a teacher by thinking about a skill or concept they learned in an earlier grade and a way they can work together as a group to teach it to younger students. They can create a lesson plan, including either a book or anchor chart. For example, second grade students can design an alphabet book for a kindergarten class, and a fifth grade group might create a place value anchor chart for second grade students.
- Students can imagine what it might be like to be an architect and work together to design a house. *The Future Architect's Handbook* by Barbara Beck (Schiffer, 2014) should be made available so students can see the entire process of planning and designing a house. They should write about all the practical components they think they will need as well as any original ideas they have. They can provide a sketch to go along with their writing or make a model using recyclable boxes and other materials.
- Students eight years and older can explore the history of medicine and find out about exciting career opportunities in the medical field by reading the book *Metamorphosis of Medicine* (Time for Kids Nonfiction Readers) by Sharon Coan (Teacher Created Materials, 2017). They should research all and choose one medical career as a group to present information on. They can write a book titled *A Day in the Life of* _____ depending on the medical career they choose to highlight. Students younger than eight years old will appreciate the book *I Want to Be a Doctor* by Laura Driscoll (HarperCollins, 2018) and can respond to it by creating their own book, making sure to include all the doctors mentioned in the text.
- Students age eight and up can read *All in a Day's Work: Police Officer* (Time for Kids Nonfiction Readers) by Diana Herweck (Teacher Created Materials, 2013) and write reports about a typical day in the police academy and what it's like to work a day in the field as an officer. Younger students can create picture books to show what they have learned about being a police officer after reading *Busy People: Police Officer* by Lucy M. George (QEB, 2016).

Literature Suggestions

- *Action! Making Movies* (Time for Kids Nonfiction Readers) by Sarah Garza (Teacher Created Materials, 2013)
- *Enhancing Engineering* (Time for Kids Nonfiction Readers) by Wendy Conklin (Teacher Created Materials, 2017)
- *STEM Careers: Reinventing Robotics* (Time Nonfiction Readers) by Saskia Lacey (Teacher Created Materials, 2017)
- *Today I'm a Veterinarian* by Marisa Polansky (Farrar, Straus and Giroux, 2018)

- *Workers Who Take Care of Me* (Time for Kids Nonfiction Readers) by Sharon Coan (Teacher Created Materials, 2015)
- *National Geographic Readers: Helpers in Your Neighborhood* (Pre-reader) by Shira Evans (National Geographic Children's Books, 2018)

LITERACY CENTER 11: THEATER CENTER

Objective

Students will engage in dramatic play and creative role-playing experiences that enhance reading comprehension and foster communication skills.

Materials

- Paper
- Writing supplies

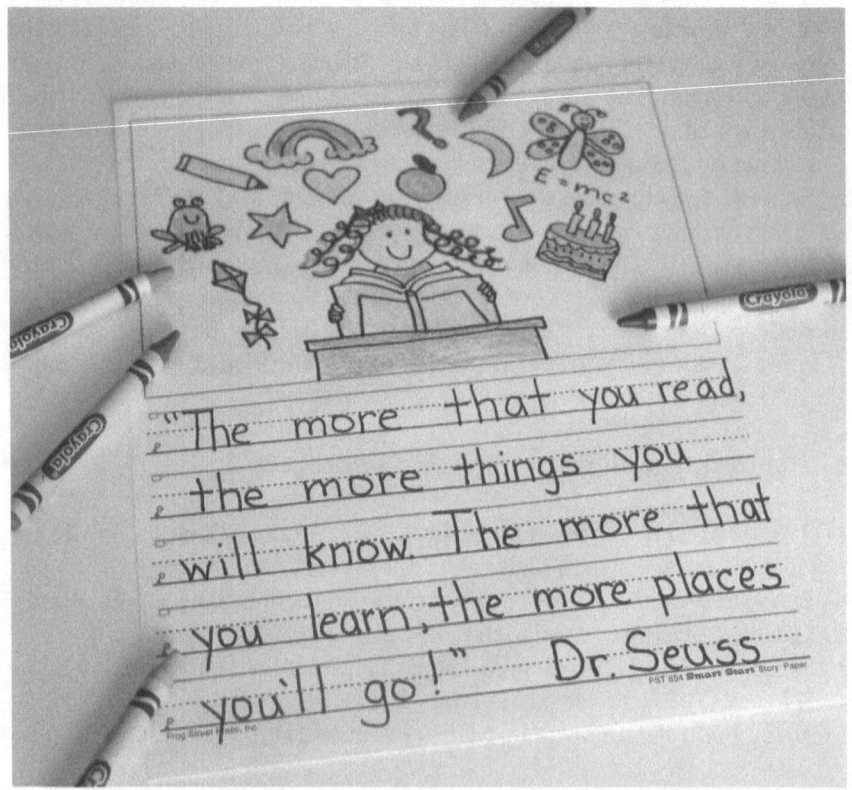

- Art supplies
- Poster board
- Everyday objects and clothing items to be used as props and costumes
- Prepared scripts
- Sets of index cards with vocabulary words, science concepts, and character names
- Stories related to a social studies theme (e.g., during a unit on the American Revolution, a book such as *Liberty or Death: The American Revolution: 1763–1783* by Betsy Maestro [HarperCollins, 2005] would be perfect)
- Folktales
- Fairy tales
- Puppets and puppet-making supplies such as popsicle sticks, googly eyes, socks, and brown paper bags

Activities

- Students can choose their favorite part of a story, show, or movie and turn it into a script. They can work as a team to write lines for each character and take turns playing the different parts. Students should also be encouraged to use poster board to make scenery and other art supplies and props to bring their show to life.
- Students can use premade puppets or create their own puppets out of art supplies (paper, and popsicle sticks, socks and googly eyes, brown paper bags and crayons) to retell folktales and fairy tales. They should decide together on a folktale or fairy tale they all enjoy and work together to write down lines that make sense to reenact the story.
- Teachers can provide a box with vocabulary words written on index cards, adding to it or rotating card as units of study change. Students can take turns choosing a word from the box and acting it out for the rest of the small group for a game of vocabulary charades.
- Teachers can provide a box with science concepts previously taught written on index cards. The selection of cards should grow as new science units and topics are studied. Students can work in their cooperative group to prepare a skit for a chosen science topic and act it out for the whole class at a later date.
- Teachers and students can create index cards with character names written on them and put them in a designated box. Students can take turns choosing characters to act out for the other group members to guess for a game of character charades.
- Students can read a book that is connected to a social studies theme they are studying, create a script, add props and scenery, and act it out for the class.

- Students can pretend to be part of a talk show that is interviewing a character from a book. Someone in the cooperative work group can be the talk show host, someone can be the chosen book character, and the other members of the group can be audience members, asking the character even more questions.
- Students can compare and contrast two fairy tales or folktales. They can then work together to create their own original play, combining characters and elements from each. For example, they might create a show with Snow White and Cinderella becoming friends or Johnny Appleseed and Paul Bunyan working together to accomplish a big task.

Literature Suggestions

- Reader's Theater: Folk and Fairy Tales English Set (Classroom Library Collections) by Teacher Created Materials (Teacher Created Materials, 2011)
- *On Stage Theater Games and Activities for Kids* by Lisa Bany-Winters (Chicago Review Press, 2012)
- *Acting Scenes and Monologues for Kids! Original Scenes and Monologues Combined into One Very Special Book!* by Bo Kane (Burbank, 2010)
- *Cinderella Outgrows the Glass Slipper and Other Zany Fractured Fairy Tale Plays* by Joan M. Wolf (Teaching Resources, 2002)
- *Kids Are So Dramatic Monologues: Volume 1* by Tracey Ann Ball (CreateSpace, 2015)
- *American Tall Tales* by Mary Pope Osborne (Knopf Books for Young Readers, 1991)

LITERACY CENTER 12: PIONEER LIFE CENTER

Objective

Students will compare and contrast life in different time periods, using a variety of resources, and applying grade-level knowledge of spelling, grammar, and usage.

Materials

- Paper
- Writing supplies
- Art supplies such as markers, paint, paintbrushes, and colored pencils

- Books about people who lived long ago (see suggested literature and titles listed in each individual activity)
- Paper bag
- Venn diagram graphic organizer template
- Construction paper and butcher paper
- Scissors
- Glue
- 1 small empty milk carton per child
- Several pretzel sticks per child
- United States map template
- Heavy cream
- Salt
- Crackers
- 1 small jar (baby food jars work well) per student

Activities

- Students can read or listen to a recording of *Daily Life in a Covered Wagon* by Paul Erickson (Puffin Books, 1997) and create their own diary entries, pretending to be children in 1853, heading west in search of a new life. Teachers should ask students to include the food they ate, how they survived sickness, and what they did when threatened by cattle thieves. The diary entries can be compiled into a class book or displayed on a bulletin board in the pioneer center.
- Students can read or listen to a recording of *A Kid's Life during the Westward Expansion* (How Kids Lived) by Sarah Machajewski (Powerkids Press, 2015) and make a list of the interesting chores and activities the pioneers engaged in while living life on the western frontier. They can then write each of the items on the list on small pieces of paper, put them in a paper bag, and take turns choosing different ones to act out so other team members might guess what the activities are. Students may also discuss how the chores and activities are similar and different from what people do today and complete a Venn diagram chart to display the comparisons to share with the rest of the class.
- Students can read or listen to a recording of *If You Traveled West in a Covered Wagon* by Ellen Levine (Scholastic Paperbacks, 1992) and discuss the differences between how people in the past dressed and how we dress today. They can then make pioneer people and clothing out of construction paper and write about the similarities and differences in the clothing they created and what they wear today.
- Students can read or listen to a recording of *Abraham Lincoln: From the Log Cabin to the White House: Campfire Heroes Line* (Campfire Graphic Novels, 2013) by Lewis Helfand and construct their own log cabins out of

small milk cartons, pretzel sticks, construction paper, and glue. Each student can glue pretzels on the sides of the milk carton so that they look like logs. To make a roof, they can then cut a square from construction paper, fold it in half, and cover each side of that with pretzels and glue it to the top of the carton. The students can work together to decide any other details and props they might want to add to their log cabins based on what they read or listened to from the book.

- Students can read or listen to a recording of *Journey of a Pioneer* by Patricia J. Murphy (DK Children, 2008) and work together as a group to fill in a blank U.S. map template to accurately show the path that was traveled along the Oregon Trail. They can also collaborate to write and illustrate a story that tells some of the things that were done while families traveled west.
- Students can read or listen to *The Quilt Story* by Tony Johnston (Puffin Books, 1996) and work together to create their own quilt that represents each member of the cooperative group. They can use precut shapes or create their own shapes out of construction paper. They can form designs on squares of white paper and then glue the squares to a larger piece of butcher paper. Students should write about why they chose the colors and shapes they did and how it feels to make something that will be part of a larger project to represent the group. Once the quilts for each team visiting the center are complete, teachers may wish to put them together to represent the whole class.
- Students can read or listen to a recording of *Pioneer Cat* (A Stepping Stone Book) by William H. Hooks (Random House Books, 1988) and create a story time line, showing the sequence of events Kate, Rosie, and Snuggs encounter as they travel to Oregon. Students can make their time line on a large piece of butcher paper that can be shared with the whole class at a later time or displayed on a bulletin board in the pioneer life center for all to see.
- Students can work together to make butter by following an authentic pioneer recipe and then write about their cooking experience. Teachers should take the time to discuss how people in the past had to churn their own butter and show the students what a butter churn looks like. *The Little House Cookbook: Frontier Foods from Laura Ingalls Wilder's Classic Stories* by Barbara M. Walker (HarperCollins, 1989) has great illustrations of a butter churn in use as well as many other authentic pioneer cooking tools and recipes.

Teachers need to prepare for this center activity by allowing the whipping cream to sit at room temperature, writing out the recipe so it's easily understood by all, and making sure all other ingredients and tools (salt, glass jars with lids, crackers) are ready and available. Students need to measure and pour one-quarter of the heavy cream into their jar and add a little salt. They need to then shake the jars for at least fifteen minutes before the cream will begin to solidify. Once it is ready, they can spread it on the crackers and taste. Students should discuss the process and taste and write about their experience as a group.

Literature Suggestions

- *If You Were a Kid on the Oregon Trail* by Josh Gregory (C. Press/F. Watts Trade, 2016)
- *A Kid's Life during the Westward Expansion* (How Kids Lived) by Sarah Machajewki (Powerkids Press, 2015)
- *Pioneer Days: Discover the Past with Fun Projects, Games, Activities, and Recipes* (American Kids in History) by David C. King (Scholastic, 2000)
- *Charlie the Ranch Dog: Charlie's Snow Day* by Ree Drummond (Harper-Collins, 2013)
- *Your Life as a Pioneer on the Oregon Trail* (The Way It Was) by Jessica Gunderson (Picture Window Books, 2012)
- *Heading West: Life with the Pioneers, 21 Activities* (For Kids) by Pat McCarthy (Chicago Review Press, 2009)

LITERACY CENTER 13: OUTER SPACE CENTER

Objective

Students will have opportunities to discover and explore outer space in a collaborative way by using a variety of resources and applying grade-level knowledge of grammar and usage. They will engage in activities that build on what they read and learn and foster oral language development.

Materials

- Paper
- Writing supplies
- Art supplies such as markers, paint, paintbrushes, colored pencils
- Butcher paper
- Large appliance box that can be used to make a spaceship for a few students to sit in and read while at the center
- Books about outer space (see suggested literature list and titles listed within activities)
- One large grocery bag for each child
- Aluminum foil

- One small plastic bag, one tablespoon plus two teaspoons instant pudding, and one tablespoon plus two teaspoons powdered milk for each child
- Measuring cups
- Measuring spoons
- Water, about half a cup per child
- Venn diagram template
- Maps and globes
- A teacher-created, student-created, or commercially produced diagram of the solar system

Activities

- Students can read or listen to a recording of *Midnight on the Moon* by Mary Pope Osborne (Random House Books for Young Readers, 1996) and work together to create a sequel for the chapter book.
- Students can work together to help design a spaceship out of a large appliance box. Teachers can use a sharp knife or box cutter to make a door tall enough for students to look out of, and each team can add designs and details to the spaceship that they have researched and decided on. Once the spaceship is designed, teachers may want to add a rug to make it more comfortable, and students can read books about outer space while sitting in the spaceship as a center activity option.
- Teachers should explain the challenges of living and working in outer space where everything must be brought in aboard a space capsule. Because everything astronauts eat in space is freeze dried, dehydrated, or vacuum sealed in pouches, this recipe for "space pudding" is an excellent one for students to prepare and write about.

    Students can measure one tablespoon plus two teaspoons of instant pudding mix and add it to their plastic bag. They can then add one tablespoon plus two teaspoons of powdered milk to their bag and mix it all up. They then need to measure half a cup of water, add it to the bag, and close the bag, ensuring it is completely sealed. Students can squeeze, mix, and squish the pudding until it is all blended and ready to eat. Once they have a chance to taste it, the group should work together to write a report about their experience making "space pudding" and how it tasted.
- Students can design their own space helmets by cutting a hole in the front of a paper grocery bag for a face and adding aluminum foil for details. They can work together as a team to decide the best way to make their grocery bag look as authentic as possible and then write step-by-step instructions to help other students that visit the center to design their own space helmet.
- Students can read or listen to a recording of *The Space Shuttle Program* (Kid's Library of Space Exploration, Volume 9) by Kim Etingoff (Village

Earth Press, 2016) to find out about the U.S. space program. They will find out the history of space exploration and how scientists hope to travel to space in years to come. They can work together to create a report, including a time line, pictures, and why the information is meaningful to them. They should have time to present their reports and share their thoughts about the learning experience with the whole class at a later scheduled time.

- Students can study the history of rockets by reading or listening to a recording of *Spaceships and Rockets: Relive Missions to Space* (DK Readers Level 2) by DK (DK Children, 2016). They can respond by working together to create a poster to advertise a trip to space, providing information such as how the rocket blasts off, the different parts of the rocket, and what an estimated price might be. Students should be given the opportunity to share their group work and thoughts on the experience with the whole class.
- Students can study the phases of the moon by reading or listening to a recording of *The Moon Book* by Gail Gibbons (Holiday House, 1997) and creating their own questions and answers for a moon trivia game. They can work together to design a game board on butcher paper or poster board and write the questions and answers on index cards. As players spin a spinner (easily created with a paper clip and pencil) or roll a die, they can move along the board, stopping at various student-determined spots to answer questions about the moon.
- Students can compare and contrast two planets using a Venn diagram template. The books *National Geographic Little Kids First Big Book of Space* by Catherine D. Hughes (National Geographic Children's Books, 2012) and *The Planets: The Definitive Visual Guide to Our Solar System* by Robert Dinwiddie (DK, 2014) would be very helpful to students for their research on the planets they are comparing and contrasting. Cooperative work groups could be assigned different planets to ensure all are researched, and when the projects are done, students can present their work to the whole class.

Suggested Literature

- *Hello, World! Solar System* by Jill McDonald (Doubleday Books for Young Readers, 2016)
- *Planets* by Ellen Hasbrouck (Little Simon, 2001)
- *Astronomy for Kids: Planets, Stars and Constellations* by Baby Professor (Baby Professor, 2016)
- *The Wondrous Workings of Planet Earth: Understanding Our World and Its Ecosystems* by Rachel Ignotofsky (Ten Speed Press, 2018)

- *First Space Encyclopedia: A Reference Guide to Our Galaxy and Beyond* by DK (DK First Reference, 2016)
- *Planets* (Explore My World) by Becky Baines (National Geographic Children's Books, 2016)

LITERACY CENTER 14: ANIMAL RESEARCH CENTER

Objective

Students will read a wide variety of sources for the purpose of learning about animals. They will apply grade-level knowledge of grammar and usage while working together to research and write about different animal topics.

Materials

- Paper (a variety of types and sizes)
- Writing supplies
- Blank books
- Art supplies such as crayons, coloring pencils, markers, paint, and paintbrushes
- Construction paper
- Recyclable items such as shoe boxes, plastic containers, and Styrofoam pieces
- Collage and puppet-making supplies such as brown paper bags, socks, googly eyes, felt pieces, and buttons
- Nonfiction animal books (see suggested literature) to connect with activities listed

Activities

At this center, students should choose one topic at a time to research as a group and then share their findings in the form of a written report, informational picture book, diorama, puppet, or any other creative way the group decides on. Each time a group enters the center, they should choose a different topic and method of displaying the information. The teacher should state the expectations of what the finished group work requires, letting the students know how much written work and information is needed, and remind students to use their knowledge of proper grammar and usage.

- Topic 1: Choose any animal. Find out what the animal looks like; what it eats; where it lives; and the animal's behavior, life cycle, and life span. Include two interesting facts about your animal and your opinion of the animal. Be sure to support your opinion with a reason.

- Topic 2: Compare and contrast information about different kinds of fish. Where do they come from? What body parts do they have? What types of water do they live in? How do they get their food? How do they defend themselves against enemies? What is true about sharks? What are the different types of sharks?
- Topic 3: What can you find out about amphibians? What do they look like, and where do they live? What are the different types of amphibians, and what do they eat? How do they protect themselves? How are frogs and toads different?
- Topic 4: What can you find out about reptiles? What do they look like, and where do they live? What are the different types of reptiles, and what do they eat? How do they protect themselves? What climates do they prefer?
- Topic 5: What is an insect? What are the different body parts of an insect, and how do they function? What do they eat, and how do they protect themselves? What stages do insects go through to reach adulthood?
- Topic 6: What are spiders? What are the parts of a spider's body, and what type of animal is it? What do they eat, and how do they defend themselves against enemies? Where do they live, and what are their webs used for?
- Topic 7: Who grows feathers? What is true about birds? What are their characteristics, and what do they eat? How do they protect themselves from enemies, and where do they live?
- Topic 8: How long ago did dinosaurs live? What different kinds of dinosaurs existed? What did they look like? What did they eat, and where did they live? How did they move? Why are they now extinct?

Suggested Literature

- *National Geographic Animal Encyclopedia: 2,500 Animals with Photos, Maps, and More!* by Lucy Spelman (National Geographic Children's Books, 2012)
- *The Animal Book: A Visual Encyclopedia of Life on Earth* by David Burnie (DK Children, 2013)
- *National Geographic Little Kids First Big Book of Animals* (National Geographic Little Kids First Big Books) by Catherine Hughes (National Geographic Children's Books, 2010)
- *Animals: A Visual Encyclopedia* (Second Edition) by DK (DK Children, 2012)
- *Ocean: A Visual Encyclopedia* by DK (DK Children, 2015)
- *Everything You Need to Know about Dinosaurs* by DK (DK Children, 2014)

LITERACY CENTER 15: BUILDING BRICK CREATIVE WRITING CENTER

Objective

Students will complete building challenges and work together to create imaginative stories, applying grade-level grammar and usage.

Materials

- Building bricks (a variety of sizes, colors, types, and boards)
- Paper
- Writing supplies
- Dictionaries and word books (see suggested literature)

Activities

Students will choose a different building challenge each time they visit this center. They must work together to complete the challenge and then write an original imaginative story based on the character and setting of their creation. Students must include more characters and a problem and a solution, and teachers should specify how long the story is required to be. Teachers should provide level-appropriate dictionaries and word books and encourage everyone to use them. Building brick creative stories can be put together in a folder or binder and kept in the center to inspire others.

- Challenge 1: A police officer at a zoo
- Challenge 2: A bus driver in the city
- Challenge 3: A grandpa at the ice-cream shop
- Challenge 4: A puppy at the beach
- Challenge 5: A boy at a football game
- Challenge 6: A teacher at the carnival
- Challenge 7: A mom at the library
- Challenge 8: A monkey at school

Suggested Literature

- *Merriam-Webster's Elementary Dictionary* by Merriam-Webster (Merriam-Webster, 2018)
- *Merriam-Webster Children's Dictionary: Features 3,000 Photographs and Illustrations* by DK (DK Children, 2015)
- *Scholastic Children's Dictionary* by Scholastic (Scholastic, 2013)
- *Children's Illustrated Dictionary* by DK (DK Children, 2014)

- *Scholastic Pocket Dictionary of Synonyms, Antonyms, and Homonyms* by Scholastic (Scholastic Reference, 2012)
- *First Children's Dictionary: A First Reference Book for Children* by DK (DK Children, 2016)

SUMMARY

Literacy centers are wonderful opportunities for students to collaborate, be creative, use critical thinking skills, and communicate in meaningful ways. They allow students to study important topics and practice essential skills authentically. All learning experiences, such as the ideas presented in this chapter, should be relevant, engaging, and part of a risk-free, positive environment for children.

Free the child's potential, and you will transform him into the world.
—Maria Montessori

Chapter Five

Adding Flavor

*Easy Classroom Recipes that Build
Community and Teach Essential Skills*

> *Cooking with kids is not just about ingredients, recipes, and cooking. It's about harnessing imagination, empowerment, and creativity.*
> —Guy Fieri

Children will have opportunities to build self-confidence as they successfully prepare these recipes and work cooperatively in small groups. They will also develop good work habits as they carefully follow directions and learn science concepts as they discover chemical changes that occur during cooking.

Each of these recipes is meant to be made in a small group setting. Teachers should assign children to small groups ahead of time and schedule time for each group to cook with them. Learning center activities connected to the recipe theme can be organized for children to engage in while waiting for their turn to cook.

One learning center can be called "read and respond" and can include any or all of the books suggested to go along with each recipe. The children can be asked to read, retell, and dramatize the stories. It's also a great idea to ask students to create a new cover or story ending or to re-create the story with a different setting. The possibilities are endless!

Although this chapter includes ideas for a "Solve It!" and a read and respond center, there are many other possibilities for learning center activities during each cooking experience. Students can research foods from other countries, practice financial literacy skills by pretending to shop for ingredients, and pretend to be selling the food they cooked. Teachers can use their imaginations and let the interests and needs of their students inspire them so that all students are actively engaged and the entire rotation time is full of cooperative community-building experiences.

EASY CLASSROOM RECIPE 1: PERFECT PITA PIZZAS

Ingredients

- 4 whole wheat or white pita bread rounds
- 1 cup spaghetti or pizza sauce
- 1 1/2 cup (6 ounces) shredded part-skim mozzarella cheese
- 2 small zucchinis, sliced 1/4 inch thick
- 1 small carrot, peeled and sliced
- 4 cherry tomatoes, halved
- 1/2 small green pepper, sliced

Steps

- Teachers can prepare the rounds ahead of time at home or in the faculty lounge if there are cooking appliances available (next 4 steps).
- Preheat a toaster oven to 375 degrees Fahrenheit.
- Line baking sheet with foil; set aside.
- Using small scissors, carefully split each pizza round around the edge; separate to form 2 rounds.
- Place rounds, rough sides up, on prepared baking sheet. Bake 5 minutes.
- Children can spread 2 tablespoons spaghetti sauce onto each round, sprinkle with cheese, and decorate with vegetables to create faces.
- Teachers can then bake the rounds for 10–15 minutes or until cheese melts.

Makes 8 servings.

Read and Respond Literature Suggestions

- *Pete's a Pizza* by William Steig (Harper Festival, 2003)
- *The Little Red Hen (Makes a Pizza)* by Philemon Sturges (Puffin Books, 2002)
- *The Princess and the Pizza* by Mary Jane and Herm Auch (Holiday House, 2003)

Solve It!

William has 36 mini pizzas to share with 3 friends. How many pizzas will each friend get?

EASY CLASSROOM RECIPE 2: LITTLE CRITTER FUN MUNCH

Ingredients

- 1 1/2 cups animal crackers
- 1 1/2 cups cheddar or original flavor fish-shaped crackers
- 1 cup dried tart cherries
- 1 cup candy-coated chocolate candy pieces
- 1 cup honey-roasted peanuts (optional; please keep in mind that many students have food allergies)

Steps

- Put animal crackers, fish crackers, dried cherries, candy, and peanuts (if desired) in a large mixing bowl.
- Carefully stir with a spoon.
- Store in a tightly covered container at room temperature.

Makes 5 cups.

Read and Respond Literature Suggestions

- *Just Grandma and Me* (Little Critter) by Mercer Mayer (Random House Books for Young Readers, 2001)
- *The View at the Zoo* by Kathleen Long Bostrom and Guy Francis (Ideals Children's Book, 2015)
- *If I Ran the Zoo* by Dr. Seuss (Random House, 1950)

Solve It!

You have 27 pets! There are 12 fish, and the rest are cats, dogs, and hamsters. How many are not fish?

EASY CLASSROOM RECIPE 3: PINK PANCAKES

Ingredients

- 1 1/2 cups pancake batter (store-bought or prepare a favorite recipe for 12 pancakes)
- 1 package of (4 serving size) gelatin, any red flavor
- 1/2 cup chopped banana

Steps

- Students can mix prepared pancake batter and gelatin together in a medium to large bowl until it is all pink.
- They can then gently stir in bananas.
- Teachers can cook pancakes with an electric hot plate or grill, following the batter package or recipe directions.

Makes 12 pancakes.

Read and Respond Literature Suggestions

- *If You Give a Pig a Pancake* by Laura Joffe Numeroff (HarperCollins, 1998)
- *Lady Pancake and Sir French Toast* by Josh Funk and Brendan Kearney (Sterling Children's Books, 2015)
- *Pinkalicious* by Victoria Kann (HarperColllins, 2016)

Solve It!

Melissa is having a party! She has 14 pink pancakes, 21 purple pancakes, and 32 rainbow pancakes. How many pancakes does she have to share at her party?

EASY CLASSROOM RECIPE 4: MONKEY POPS

Ingredients

- 1 (14-ounce) can sweetened condensed milk
- 1 (8-ounce) container vanilla yogurt
- 2 ripe bananas
- 1/2 cup orange juice

Steps

- In blender container, combine all ingredients and blend until smooth. Stop occasionally to scrape down sides.
- Spoon banana mixture into 8 (5-ounce) paper cups. Freeze 30 minutes. Insert wooden craft sticks into the center of each cup; freeze until firm.

Makes 8 pops.

Read and Respond Literature Suggestions

- *Grumpy Monkey* by Suzanne Lang (Random House Books for Young Readers, 2018)
- *Curious George* by H. A. Rey (HMH Books for Young Readers, 2016)
- *Gorilla Loves Vanilla* by Chae Strathie (B. E. S., 2016)

Solve It!

You gave your very hungry gorilla friend 19 banana pops. Now he has 31! How many did he have before you gave him 19?

EASY CLASSROOM RECIPE 5: SWEET SUNSHINE COOKIES

Ingredients

- 3 3/4 cups sifted powdered sugar
- 3 tablespoons meringue powder
- 6 tablespoons frozen lemonade concentrate, thawed
- Ready to slice and bake cookie dough (enough so every child will have at least 1 serving)
- Thin pretzel sticks
- Yellow food coloring
- Gummy fruit and black licorice strings

Steps

- Prepare a lemon-flavored icing. Beat the powdered sugar, meringue powder, and frozen lemonade concentrate in a large bowl with electric mixer at high speed until smooth. Cover. Let stand at room temperature.
- Preheat oven according to cookie dough instructions.
- Roll dough on floured surface to 1/8-inch thickness. Cut out cookies using a 3-inch round cookie cutter.

- Place cookies on prepared cookie sheets. Place pretzel sticks into the edge of cookies to resemble sunshine rays; press gently.
- Teachers can bake cookies according to cookie dough instructions or until lightly browned. This can be done in a toaster oven if you don't have access to a traditional oven. Remove to wire racks; cool completely.
- Add food coloring to the icing. Spread icing evenly onto the cookies.
- Decorate cookies with gummy fruit and licorice strings to make faces.
- Let stand 1 hour or until dry.

Makes 20 cookies.

Read and Respond Literature Suggestions

- *Arrow to the Sun: A Pueblo Indian Tale* by Gerald McDermott (Puffin Books, 1977)
- *Sunshine Makes the Seasons* (Let's Read and Find Out) by Dr. Franklyn M. Branley (HarperCollins, 2016)
- *Sun, Sun: The Joy of a Summer Day at the Beach* by Brad Gray (CreateSpace, 2016)

Solve It!

You are at the beach and want to buy lemonade. It costs $1.50, and you have three quarters, five dimes, and a nickel. Do you have enough money?

EASY CLASSROOM RECIPE 6: KITTY CAT STRAWBERRY AMBROSIA

Ingredients

- 2 cups strawberries
- 1 pint heavy cream or yogurt
- 4 tablespoons white granulated sugar
- Grapes, chocolate chips, small cookies, wafers, and sliced kiwi fruit to create the cat face

Steps

- Teachers and older students can cut the strawberries in half and put them in a bowl. Children will love mashing them with a fork until smooth.
- Whisk the cream or yogurt until it is thick and creamy. Add this and the sugar to the mashed fruit. Stir them in well. Pour the fruit mixture into

serving dishes and decorate them to look like a kitty cat (or any type of animal). You can slice strawberries for ears, make eyes with grapes, and use a cookie or chocolate chip for a nose. Sliced kiwi makes great whiskers.

Makes 6 servings.

Read and Respond Literature Suggestions

- *Pete the Cat, I Love My White Shoes* by James Dean (HarperCollins, 2010)
- *If You Give a Cat a Cupcake* by Laura Joffe Numeroff (HarperCollins, 2008)
- *The Cat in the Hat* by Dr. Seuss (Random House, 1957)

Solve It!

Pete the Cat made 31 paper airplanes, but only 11 would fly. How many would not fly?

EASY CLASSROOM RECIPE 7: BOA CONSTRICTOR BREAD CREATIONS

Ingredients

- 1 loaf frozen bread dough, defrosted
- Flour
- Currants or raisins
- Red and green food coloring
- 1/3 cup melted margarine

Steps

- Divide the dough into 6–8 pieces. Dip each piece in flour.
- Place the dough pieces on a separate piece of aluminum foil for each child and place on a cookie sheet ahead of time.
- Students roll their piece of dough into a snake and add 2 currants or raisins for eyes.
- Add food coloring to melted margarine. Students use this as paint to create boa constrictor designs on the snakes.
- Teachers can bake the snakes in a toaster oven at 350 degrees Fahrenheit for about 15 minutes.

Makes 6–8 servings.

Read and Respond Literature Suggestions

- *The Day Jimmy's Boa Ate the Wash* by Trinka Hakes Noble (Puffin Books, 1992)
- *Crictor* by Tomi Ungerer (HarperCollins, 1983)
- *Mufaro's Beautiful Daughters* by John Steptoe (Puffin Books, 2008)

Solve It!

Jimmy's pet newborn boa constrictor is 60 centimeters long. How many more centimeters will it have to grow to measure 2 meters?

EASY CLASSROOM RECIPE 8: PIGS IN A BLANKET

Ingredients

- 3 hot dogs
- 3 ready-to-bake crescent rolls in a tube
- Catsup
- Mustard

Steps

- Teachers should cut 3 hot dogs in half.
- They can then remove 3 crescent rolls from the tube and cut each in half.
- Students can wrap half a crescent roll around each hot dog half.
- Teachers can place wrapped hot dogs on a cookie sheet. Bake at 375 degrees Fahrenheit for 15 minutes. This can easily be done in a toaster oven or on an electric grill.
- Serve with catsup and mustard for dipping.

Makes 6 servings.

Read and Respond Literature Suggestions

- *The Three Little Pigs* by Paul Galdone (HMH Books for Young Readers, 1984)
- *Pigs* by Robert Munsch (Annick Press, 1989)
- *My Lucky Day* by Keiko Kasza (Puffin Books, 2005)

Solve It!

The 3 little pigs went to work together to build a house of bricks. They measured and decided they needed 52 bricks. They only have 29 bricks. How many more bricks do they need?

EASY CLASSROOM RECIPE 9: ANY WHICH WAY SANDWICHES

Ingredients

- Bread (2 slices per child)
- A variety of spreads (peanut butter or soy nut butter, cream cheese, and any flavor of jellies and jams)
- Cookie cutters

- A variety of sandwich add-ins, such as raisins, strawberries, banana slices, and apple slices

Steps

- Encourage the children to really think about the type of sandwich they want to create.
- Chart suggestions, such as making a traditional sandwich with 2 slices of bread and a spread or 2 in the middle, and any other ideas they think of.
- Allow time for children to reflect on suggestions and plan their own idea before they start assembling any food.
- Let them finally assemble the sandwiches "any which way."
- Allow unhurried time for casual conversations while they eat their sandwiches so they can enjoy each other's company. Encourage respectful accountable talk about the similarities and differences in the sandwich creations.

Read and Respond Literature Suggestions

- *Chester's Way* by Kevin Henkes (Greenwillow Books, 1997)
- *Spider Sandwiches* by Claire Freedman (Bloomsbury USA Children's, 2014)
- *Sam's Sandwich* by David Pelham (Candlewick, 2015)

Solve It!

Kristine bought a peanut butter and jelly sandwich and received her change in several coins. The total change was $0.72. What are some possibilities of coin combinations she received?

EASY CLASSROOM RECIPE 10: LET'S PRETEND IT'S OUR BIRTHDAY CONES

Ingredients

- 2 cups cold milk
- 1 4-ounce box instant pudding mix, any flavor
- 6 flat-bottomed ice-cream cones
- Prepared whipped cream
- Candy sprinkles

Steps

- Pour 2 cups cold milk in a bowl.
- Add the instant pudding mix and beat with a wire whisk.
- Wait 10 minutes. Spoon pudding into the ice-cream cones.
- Freeze for at least 3 hours.
- Add whipped cream and candy and pretend it is everyone's birthday!

Makes 6 servings.

Read and Respond Literature Suggestions

- *Happy Birthday to You* by Dr. Seuss (Random House Books for Young Readers, 1959)
- *Happy Birthday to You, You Belong in a Zoo* by Diane deGroat (Harper-Collins, 2007)
- *Fancy Nancy: Puppy Party* by Jane O'Connor (Harper Festival, 2013)

Solve It!

Jay has 5 blue balloons, 8 red balloons, and 4 yellow balloons. Some are green. If there are 22 balloons in all, how many are green?

EASY CLASSROOM RECIPE 11: HEARTWARMING HOT COCOA

Ingredients

- 1 pound cocoa powder
- 8-quart box instant nonfat dry milk
- 6-ounce jar nondairy creamer
- 1 cup powdered sugar
- Hot water
- Mini marshmallows

Steps

- To create enough cocoa mix for 30 servings, mix the cocoa powder, dry milk, creamer, and powdered sugar in a large bowl. Store it in an airtight container.
- For 1 serving, add 6 tablespoons of the mix to 1 cup of hot water and stir well. Add marshmallows.

- As the children enjoy their drink, encourage discussion about things that "warm their hearts."

Makes 30 servings.

Read and Respond Literature Suggestions

- *The Snowy Day* by Ezra Jack Keats (Puffin Books, 1978)
- *The Magic of Friendship Snow* by Andi Cann (Mindview Press, 2018)
- *The Mitten* by Jan Brett (G. P. Putnam's Sons Books for Young Readers, 1996)

Solve It!

Marissa has 64 marshmallows to share with 4 friends. How many will each friend get?

EASY CLASSROOM RECIPE 12: EXTRA-SPECIAL STUFFED EGGS

Ingredients

- 3 eggs
- 1 tablespoon relish
- 2 tablespoons mayonnaise
- ¼ teaspoon salt
- Dash pepper
- Olives

Steps

- Teachers can prepare ahead of time by placing 3 eggs in a pan, covering with water, and boiling gently for 15 minutes.
- Older students can peel cooled eggs, cut in half with a safe plastic knife, and scoop out yolks.
- Students can use a fork to mash yolks in a small bowl.
- Teachers and students together can add relish, mayonnaise, salt, and pepper.
- Children will love filling the eggs with the yolk mixture and topping them with half an olive. Chill for about 10 minutes.
- As the children eat the "extra-special" stuffed eggs, ask them to come up with reasons their friends are "extra special."

Makes 6 servings.

Read and Respond Literature Suggestions

- *Chickens Aren't the Only Ones* by Ruth Heller (Puffin Books, 1999)

- *Horton Hatches the Egg* by Dr. Seuss (Random House Books for Young Readers, 2004)
- *Green Eggs and Ham* by Dr. Seuss (Random House, 1960)
- *Rechenka's Eggs* by Patricia Polacco (Puffin Books, 1996)

Solve It!

We bought 12 eggs for $3.00. How much did each egg cost? How much would we need to buy to double the amount of eggs next time?

EASY CLASSROOM RECIPE 13: JUST RIGHT FOR ME PORRIDGE

Ingredients

- 3 cups water
- 1/4 teaspoon salt
- 1/2 cup raisins
- 2 cups oatmeal
- 1/2 teaspoon cinnamon
- 1/4 cup sliced almonds
- Milk
- Brown sugar

Steps

- Teachers can prepare the oatmeal ahead of time in the faculty lounge by bringing water, salt, and raisins to a boil.
- Teachers should then add oatmeal, stir, and cook 5 minutes.
- Students can add cinnamon and sliced almonds. Remember that many students have food allergies.
- When the porridge is "just right," add milk, sprinkle with brown sugar, and enjoy.

Makes 6 servings.

Read and Respond Literature Suggestions

- *Goldilocks and the Three Bears* by Jan Brett (Putnam and Grosset, 1996)
- *Goldilocks and the Three Bears* by James Marshall (Picture Puffin Books, 1998)
- *The Magic Porridge Pot* by Paul Galdone (Clarion Books, 1979)

Solve It!

Baby Bear's goal is to have 43 toy cars in his collection. He has 25. How many more cars does Baby Bear need to collect?

EASY CLASSROOM RECIPE 14: FRIENDLY FRUIT SALAD

Ingredients

- Any variety of fresh or canned fruits
- 3 cups rainbow-colored mini marshmallows
- Cinnamon

Steps

- Teachers can prepare ahead of time by cutting the fruit into bite-sized pieces.
- Drain the canned fruits.
- Place each fruit in its own bowl and the marshmallows in a separate bowl.
- Give each child his or her own bowl and spoon and encourage the children to choose the fruit they prefer. Also allow them to decide whether to add marshmallows or not.
- Add a sprinkle of cinnamon and mix well.

Makes 20 servings.

Read and Respond Literature Suggestions

- *Frog and Toad Are Friends* by Arnold Lobel (Harper, 1970)
- *Same, Same but Different* by Jenny Sue Kostecki-Shaw (Henry Holt and Company, 2011)
- *We Don't Eat Our Classmates* by Ryan T. Higgins (Disney Hyperion, 2018)

Solve It!

Frog and Toad have fruit salad to share with their friends. They have 11 friends visiting, but they only have 5 cups and 6 spoons. How many more cups and spoons do they need?

EASY CLASSROOM RECIPE 15: DELICIOUS DIRT CUPS

Ingredients

- 6 whole graham crackers
- 6-ounce package instant chocolate pudding
- 3 cups cold milk
- Any type of add-in the children prefer that resembles seeds (small candy, sunflower seeds, peanuts)
- 6 gummy worms

Steps

- Put the graham crackers in a large plastic bag and crush with fingers or rolling pin.
- Put the pudding and milk in a jar and shake for 2 minutes.
- Pour pudding into 6 cups.
- Stir in crushed graham crackers.
- Ask students to use spoons to dig holes for "seeds" and gummy worms.

Makes 6 servings.

Read and Respond Literature Suggestions

- *Planting a Rainbow* by Lois Ehlert (HMH Books for Young Readers, 1992)
- *The Carrot Seed* by Ruth Krause (Scholastic, 1945)
- *Tops and Bottoms* by Janet Stevens (Harcourt Brace, 1995)

Solve It!

Our class planted 26 seeds. Another class planted half that many seeds. How many seeds were planted altogether?

Cooking is love made visible.

—Anonymous

Chapter Six

Embracing STEM Education

Fifteen Collaborative Group Activities to Inspire Critical-Thinking Skills, Communication, and Creativity

> *Scientists discover the way the world exists; engineers create the world that never was.*
>
> —Theodore Von Karman

STEM is the acronym for science, technology, engineering, and math and describes an interdisciplinary approach to learning where academic concepts are matched with real-world problem-solving challenges. Students are encouraged to communicate, collaborate, use critical-thinking skills, and be creative when teachers implement STEM education into their curriculum.

STEM is not meant to be a separate part of the school day. STEM can be easily integrated into every subject. Any lesson or content matter can be transformed into a STEM activity, or challenge, by planning ways for students to solve problems in creative ways. STEM education is not about doing a lot of science experiments or providing hands-on activities in a classroom. STEM education involves both problem-based and performance-based innovative activities that allow students to think outside the box and may even spark a passion for a future career in a STEM field.

STEM integration, as seen in every one of the collaborative group challenges presented in this chapter, is effective when it includes the following components:

- A meaningful problem to solve
- Collaboration among students
- A design challenge

- Communication of process and findings
- Reflection
- Redesign

Before presenting STEM collaborative group challenges to a class, rules should be established and posted so they are clear and accessible to all. These are some simple STEM rule suggestions:

- Use all materials respectfully.
- Stay on task.
- Work until time is up. (Reflect and redesign if done.)

Separate from rules, students will benefit from having a standard set of guidelines, such as these, to follow when working through the STEM challenge process:

- Ask: What are the constraints? What have others done?
- Imagine: What are some solutions? Brainstorm ideas. Choose the best idea.
- Plan: Think. Sketch. Label. Make a list of materials.
- Create: Make a model and test it.
- Improve: Reflect and share findings. Make changes to make your design better.
- Retest.

Many teachers provide students with a STEM journal or folder to keep ideas, creations, reflections, and redesigns in one place. STEM challenge plans can be completed on a plain piece of paper; however, some teachers find it helpful to create a STEM challenge template with the students' abilities and needs in mind. It can be as simple as providing spaces for a plan, design, and redesign for younger students and more complex with greater expectations and reflection prompts for advanced students to consider and respond to.

STEM notebooks, whether they are comprised of blank pages or teacher-made templates, are valuable when used as authentic assessment pieces for goal setting and communicating STEM education to families.

It is recommended for teachers to have an area designated in their classroom for STEM supplies. There should be a place for materials that students bring into the classroom, such as a bucket, bin, labeled shelf, or a space in a closet. Materials that are used frequently, such as glue sticks, scissors, markers, and tagboard, need to be in an area that is accessible to all students without adults needing to assist.

Materials should be organized in such a way that students understand how to return them correctly. Labels with pictures on them are very efficient, and having a color-coded system to keep similar types of materials together is a great idea. Many teachers find it useful to have a "lost and found" bin for glue stick lids, found pencils, and other random pieces.

STEM education is highly engaging, and many challenges will require several sessions. Because of this it is important to teach students how to stop working, clean up in an organized way, and record their progress as they end each session. Students should each have a designated spot to keep their work in progress and materials they are working with. Some teachers have a table or shelf space labeled with each child's name (or cooperative group name) just for that purpose. This encourages students to not worry and be so quick to "finish" because they know their work will be safe and there will be other opportunities to redesign and perfect their project.

Students need to understand the role of the teacher throughout these activities and challenges. STEM learning is meant to be student centered. Instead of automatically presenting students with the information they need to learn, students should be planning, creating, and solving, while the teacher's role is to monitor and provide feedback.

These STEM challenges are meant to be implemented as cooperative group work. It's important for teachers to teach, model, and display appropriate ways for students to communicate to ensure work is meaningful and the learning is authentic. Raising the level of discourse during STEM education is extremely important for students at every level.

These discussion prompts are effective for encouraging smart STEM talk:

- I agree with _____ because . . .
- I disagree with _____ because . . .
- Could you please explain more about . . .
- I would like to add on to that idea . . .
- I was confused about . . .
- This reminds me of . . .
- I was wondering about . . .
- Another idea I had was . . .

STEM ACTIVITY 1: CAMPING CHAOS

Challenge

Create a shelter for a group of friends (cut-out paper people) that will keep them dry if it rains while they are out camping. Use five or fewer of the different building supplies available. Water will be dripped onto the shelter to test whether or not it will keep the friends dry.

Materials

- Paper
- Paper plates
- Wax paper
- Aluminum foil
- Paper towel tubes
- Scotch tape
- Pipe cleaners
- Craft sticks
- Straws
- Scissors
- Paper and writing supplies or STEM journal to record building plans

Steps

Students work in groups of three or four. They will first create a group of four paper friends by drawing them and cutting them out of paper. They will then decide as a team which building supplies they are going to use for their structure. Students need to devise a plan and work by trial and error to meet the challenge until they are happy with their shelter. The group should be able to share their strategies and ideas with the class and prove that the shelter is effective in keeping the paper friends dry when water is dripped onto the shelter.

STEM ACTIVITY 2: TEAMWORK REQUIRED CUP PYRAMID

Challenge

Build a pyramid with all twenty-five plastic cups using only the rubber-band tool.

Materials

- 25 (16-ounce) plastic cups
- 1 rubber band
- 1 12-inch piece of string tied to the rubber band for each member of the cooperative group
- Paper and writing supplies or STEM journal to record ideas and plan

Steps

Students work in groups of three to eight. Each group needs to stand in a circle with everyone holding a piece of string (which has been tied to the rubber band). The students need to pull on their strings to expand the rubber band and then move in together to shrink the rubber band around the cups, so they are using the band to pick up the cups. They will most likely need to make several attempts and adjustments of their process until they are able to build a pyramid with all twenty-five cups.

More advanced students might be given just the materials and the challenge while beginners may be shown how to use the already-assembled rubber-band tool. Students should be able to discuss what made this task challenging and how they changed their methods based on their results while attempting this pyramid-building challenge.

STEM ACTIVITY 3: MARSHMALLOW ON TOP

Challenge

Build the tallest freestanding structure you can out of spaghetti. Use only the materials provided, and complete the challenge in 22 minutes (adjust time depending on students' age and ability). The marshmallow needs to be on top.

Materials

- 20 sticks of spaghetti
- 1 yard of tape
- 1 yard of string
- 1 marshmallow
- Timer
- Paper and writing supplies or STEM journal to record building plans

Steps

Students work in groups of four to six. Once all groups are given the challenge and supplies, the timer can be set for 22 minutes (or adjusted time), and students will work together to design, redesign, and reflect on their work until the time is up. Once the time is up, the groups will report to the class about their strategies and reasons why they either were able to meet the challenge or why they did not meet the challenge. If they were not successful, they will tell what they would do differently the next time.

STEM ACTIVITY 4: RECYCLE TO THE TOP

Challenge

Using only paper, build a structure as tall as you can. Students may be timed, depending on their age and ability, allowing five to fifteen minutes to complete the challenge.

Materials

- Paper
- Timer
- Paper and writing supplies or STEM journal to record building plans

Steps

Students work in groups of three or four to brainstorm ideas, choose the best idea, and devise a plan that will help them build the tallest structure they can using only paper. They will then carry out the plan, attempting as a team to complete the challenge. When the time is up, they will report their team strategies, successes, and challenges to the whole class. Younger students may be shown how folding or rolling the paper can be effective once first attempts of this challenge have been made. All teams should discuss how they can improve their structure and then be given additional time to redesign.

STEM ACTIVITY 5: A-MAZING RACE

Challenge

Using play dough and Q-tips, design a maze that will allow a ping-pong ball to travel from one side of a cookie sheet to the other.

Materials

- Play dough
- Q-tips
- Cookie sheet
- Ping-pong ball
- Paper and writing supplies or STEM journal to record plans

Steps

Students work together in groups of three or four to complete the challenge with only the materials listed. They will brainstorm ideas and choose the best idea as a group. Students will draw a picture and write a step-by-step plan of how they want their maze to be built. As a group, they will then create, improve, and reflect on their work. They will present their completed mazes to the class, discussing their strategies and trial-and-error process. It's important for students to talk about the challenges they faced, ways the maze might be improved, or how they might work more effectively the next time.

STEM ACTIVITY 6: BALLOON TOWER CHALLENGE

Challenge

Build the tallest freestanding tower you can using only a bag of balloons and masking tape. Students may be timed for twelve to twenty minutes (depending on age and ability) to keep the students focused on building.

Materials

- Bag of balloons
- Masking tape
- Measurement tools
- Paper and writing supplies or STEM journal to record building plans

Steps

Students work together in groups of three or four to blow up balloons and decide how they are going to hold them together for a tower. Students may need to be reminded about the importance of a sturdy base and to pay attention to the time constraint. When time is up, students should discuss how their team completed the challenge, including any obstacles they encountered and what they might do differently next time. The teacher and students will also measure the towers and discuss differences and similarities in structures.

STEM ACTIVITY 7: POM-POM DROP

Challenge

Construct a pom-pom drop that can keep a "ball" going for more than ten seconds. A pom-pom drop is simply a structure that a pom-pom can roll through. Students might tape cardboard rolls to a wall or window to allow the

pom-pom to roll through and experiment by cutting the rolls in half or by cutting openings in them.

Materials

- Paper towel rolls
- Toilet paper rolls
- Washi tape
- Pom-poms
- Other types of small balls, such as marbles or bouncy balls
- Paper and writing supplies or STEM journal to record plans

Steps

Students work in groups of three to five to construct a pom-pom drop that will keep a "ball" going for more than ten seconds. This will require testing different designs (created from rolls and tape) and materials (balls). As the students create, the teacher should encourage students to adjust and add to their drop. The concept of gravity can be discussed as students experiment to see how sizes and weights of materials affect how quickly they fall.

STEM ACTIVITY 8: PAPER AIRPLANE CHALLENGE

Challenge

Make a paper airplane that can carry cargo (coins) and glide more than ten feet.

Materials

- Construction paper
- Tape
- Coins
- "How-to" books on the art of creating paper airplanes, such as:
  - *Kids' Paper Airplane Book* by Ken Blackburn (Workman, 1996)
  - *Ultimate Paper Airplanes for Kids* by Andrew Dewar (Tuttle, 2015)

Steps

Students work together in groups of three or four to construct a paper airplane that will carry coins and glide at least ten feet. They first need to know how to make a paper airplane. There are several books available that students can use as a guide if they have never done this before. They then decide which coins to use and the most effective way to position them so the plane will glide at least ten feet. This will take lots of trial and error, and students should share their small-group experience with the whole class, discussing successes, challenges, and ways they would improve their design and strategies in the future.

STEM ACTIVITY 9: FAIRY-TALE HOUSE CONSTRUCTION

Challenge

Construct a fairy-tale house that can stand on its own. It must include graham crackers for the structure, frosting for the glue, and at least four decorative candy elements.

Materials

- Graham crackers
- Frosting
- Marshmallows
- Gumdrops
- Candy canes
- Sprinkles
- M&Ms
- Paper and writing supplies or STEM journal for creating building plans

Steps

Students work together in groups of three or four to brainstorm, plan, create, and improve on their fairy-tale house construction. They will brainstorm how they will build their house by deciding on materials and drawing a diagram of their intended creation. They will work together to follow the plan and build the house. Reflection is an important part of this challenge. After small groups of students reflect, they should be able to report to the whole class about the best part of their fairy-tale house, what could be better, and ways it could be improved in the future.

STEM ACTIVITY 10: NEWSPAPER FORT CHALLENGE

Challenge

Build a newspaper fort your whole group can fit in.

Materials

- Newspaper
- Tape
- Stapler
- Paper and writing supplies or STEM journal for recording building plans

Steps

Students work in groups of two or three and decide together on a building plan. They will brainstorm how they are going to manipulate the newspaper and how they will use either tape or a stapler to successfully hold it together. Students will decide on the best idea, draw a picture of it, and finally build the fort. Once the fort is complete, they must sit inside it, discuss ways in which it was successful, how it could be improved, and what they would do differently in the future. Each cooperative small group should share their strategies and reflections with the whole class.

STEM ACTIVITY 11: FUNCTIONAL AND CREATIVE CARDBOARD CHALLENGE

Challenge

Create something out of cardboard that is both creative and functional.

Materials

- Cardboard recyclables such as boxes, scraps, tubes, and sheets
- Glue, tape, scissors, stapler
- Art supplies such as markers, colored pencils, and paint

Steps

Students work in groups of two or three and decide together on something they would like to construct that is functional and creative. They need to

think carefully about the materials and brainstorm possibilities. Once they choose the best idea, they can make a step-by-step plan by drawing a picture and listing materials. They will work together to create the design, test it, and decide how it can be improved. Each small group will present their functional and creative masterpiece to the class, demonstrating its function and sharing their strategies, reflections, and ideas for the future.

STEM ACTIVITY 12: PAPER CHAIN CHALLENGE

Challenge

Construct the longest paper chain using only one piece of construction paper.

Materials

- 1 piece of construction paper
- Scissors
- Glue

Steps

Students work in groups of three or four to carefully plan how they are going to build their paper chain because they only have one paper and cannot ask for a replacement piece. They will brainstorm ideas, choose the best one, and make a plan. A time can be set (fifteen to thirty minutes) based on the age and ability of the students. Once the time is called, the chains will be placed beside each other to determine which chain is the longest. Each cooperative small group will discuss their plans and strategies with the entire class. They will also discuss ways in which they were successful and things they could improve on in the future.

STEM ACTIVITY 13: JUST INDEX CARDS CHALLENGE

Challenge

Create the tallest freestanding tower you can in the allotted time with just index cards. The index cards may be folded, torn, crumpled, or manipulated in any way, but no scissors, tape, glue, or any other construction tool at all is allowed.

Materials

- Index cards
- Paper and writing supplies or STEM journal for recording building plans

Steps

Students work in groups of three or four and decide together on the best way to create their tower using only index cards. Once they decide on the best idea, they can draw a picture and make a step-by-step plan. They will then create their tower, improving on their design as needed. Once the set time (fifteen to thirty minutes) is up, towers should be measured, and cooperative groups should discuss strategies, challenges, and ideas for future improvements with the whole class.

STEM ACTIVITY 14: SWING SET CHALLENGE

Challenge

Construct a swing set for a small toy figure. It must have a swing mechanism that works and a seat that fits the toy figure securely.

Materials

- Toy figure
- Craft sticks
- Cardboard tubes
- Pipe cleaners
- Cups
- Rubber bands
- Craft foam
- Aluminum foil
- Building bricks
- Glue
- Brads or paper fasteners
- Scissors
- Stapler, staples
- Paper and writing supplies or STEM journal to create building plans

Steps

Students work in groups of three or four to brainstorm ideas, choose the best idea, and come up with a construction plan to build a working swing set that will securely fit a given toy figure. They will draw a picture of their idea and develop a step-by-step plan together. Once they create, test, and reflect on the design, they should share their swing set construction with the entire class. It is important for students to discuss strategies, successes, and ways they could improve on their method and design in the future.

STEM ACTIVITY 15: BUILDING BRICK SCHOOL SUPPLY CADDY CHALLENGE

Challenge

Construct a school supply caddy out of only building bricks. The caddy should hold five pencils, five highlighters, and five boxes of eight crayons (adapt this to fit supply needs of students).

Materials

- Building bricks
- School supplies that will need to fit in the caddy
- Paper and writing supplies or STEM journal for recording building plans

Steps

Students work in groups of three to five to brainstorm ideas about how they can most effectively construct a school supply caddy out of building bricks that will hold all the necessary supplies. They will choose the best idea, draw a picture, and devise a step-by-step plan. Once they create, test, improve, and reflect on their construction, the group should then share their strategies, group successes, and plans for future improvements.

Collaboration and interaction are necessary in STEM learning experiences. When teachers provide consistent modeling of effective communication and opportunities for students to engage in rich academic discourse, students will be better prepared to apply new learning in creative and innovative ways.

Creativity is thinking up new things. Innovation is doing new things.
—Theodore Levitt

Chapter Seven

The Power of the Author Study

Fifteen Shared Reading Experiences to Encourage Communication and Build Critical-Thinking Skills in Your Classroom

> There are many little ways to enlarge your child's world. Love of books is the best of all.
>
> —Jacqueline Kennedy

Building a community of readers, establishing closer connections, and fostering a love of books are important goals for teachers who want to inspire authentic learning, collaboration, better communication, and improved literacy skills in their classroom. Exposing students to a variety of authors, and providing rich, engaging literacy experiences that will allow them to reflect and respond to the authors' work, will ensure that meaningful learning takes place and that a love of books is encouraged.

This chapter includes a variety of wonderful authors that will spark students' interests and help them grow as readers and writers. Teachers can choose authors that they think are most appropriate for their classes based on the level, expertise, and interests of their students. It would be great to create a special space in the classroom dedicated to the author study. Some teachers like to put together a trifold board with pictures of the author, information about the author's life, and graphic organizers displaying story elements that students can add to throughout the author study.

There are four books suggested for each author. Teachers might choose to plan their author studies to last a month, dedicating a week to each book. It is recommended that teachers read each suggested book for the author they are studying in an interactive, expressive way and allow time for students to answer and ask questions about each one. Some teachers find it helpful for students to keep a journal to answer questions in or as a place to record their feelings and thoughts. The journal might also serve as an assessment piece and a great way to give families a glimpse into their child's learning at a parent/teacher conference.

The listed projects for each author are great opportunities for students to work in small groups to collaborate, use critical-thinking skills, and reflect on and respond to the author study experience. The projects are meant to be worked on throughout the author study and presented as a culmination project.

As always, it is important that students are reminded of group work expectations and to use proper accountable talk while collaborating and communicating. Students should be encouraged to be creative and thoughtful about listening to each other's ideas when working on the project. There should be time for each group to share their project and discuss successes and challenges they experienced throughout the process with the whole class.

SHARED READING EXPERIENCE 1: CELEBRATING CHANGE WITH ERIC CARLE

Author

Eric Carle

Grade-Level Recommendation

PreK–Grade 1

Books

- *Draw Me a Star* (Puffin Books, 1998)
- *The Mixed-Up Chameleon* (Harper Festival, 1998)
- *The Grouchy Ladybug* (Harper Festival, 1999)
- *A House for a Hermit Crab* (Simon and Schuster Books for Young Readers, 1991)

Materials

- Paper or journal and writing/drawing supplies for note-taking and planning
- Colorful tissue paper
- White construction paper
- Clear glue and paintbrushes for application

- Scissors
- Yarn
- Plastic hanger

Project

Throughout the author study, after each of the books is read, students should work together in their small cooperative groups to discuss the changes that occurred in each of the stories. They can collect ideas in a journal or on paper they can refer to and add to as each of the four books is read and discussed. Students should also discuss and record their thoughts about the beautiful tissue paper collage-style artwork Eric Carle uses in each book.

Students will create their own representations of the tissue-paper collage pictures as they put together a mobile that shows changes that have occurred within each member of the group. Each child needs to cut a shape out of white construction paper that represents a change he or she has experienced. Maybe students have moved to a new house, learned to ride a bike, or have a new baby sibling. Their shape needs to somehow show the change. They can then paint a layer of clear glue over the shape, apply colorful cut or torn tissue paper pieces, and attach it to a plastic hanger.

Once every member of the group attaches his or her artwork, the mobile can be hung in the author study center or classroom library. Each small group of children should have the opportunity to explain to the whole class why they chose the shapes they did and how they felt about their author study experience.

SHARED READING EXPERIENCE 2: CELEBRATING THE ALPHABET

Author

Laura Joffe Numeroff

Grade-Level Recommendation

PreK–Grade 1

Books

- *If You Give a Mouse a Cookie* (HarperCollins, 2015)
- *If You Give a Pig a Party* (HarperCollins, 2005)
- *If You Give a Cat a Cupcake* (HarperCollins, 2008)
- *If You Give a Moose a Muffin* (HarperCollins, 1991)

Materials

- Paper
- Writing supplies such as pencils, colored pencils
- Art supplies such as construction paper, scissors, glue, crayons, markers
- ABC books and charts
- Animal books
- Play dough or clay
- One shallow box for each cooperative group

Project

Throughout the author study, and after each of the books is read, students should work together in their cooperative small groups to discuss the characters and cause/effect events that occurred in each story. They should also be given time to think about other animals and things other animals might ask for as if they were going to create a book in the style of Laura Joffe Numeroff. Have them brainstorm and list animals and foods to represent every letter of the alphabet with the help of ABC books and animal books.

Students can use play dough or clay to create an animal sculpture display. Each animal should hold a particular food or object that has the same beginning sound as the name of the animal. Students can add background details with construction paper and other art supplies and keep the display in a shallow box with labels for each letter of the alphabet. Cooperative groups can be given the opportunity to share and discuss their work and also talk about successes and challenges they experienced throughout the project.

SHARED READING EXPERIENCE 3:
CREATING SMALL MOMENTS WITH EZRA JACK KEATS

Author

Ezra Jack Keats

Grade-Level Recommendation

PreK–Grade 1

Books

- *The Snowy Day* (Puffin Books, 1976)
- *Peter's Chair* (Puffin Books, 1998)
- *Pet Show!* (Puffin Books, 2001)

- *A Letter to Amy* (Puffin Books, 1998)

Materials

- Paper
- Journal (optional)
- Writing supplies such as pencils, colored pencils
- Art supplies such as construction paper, scissors, glue, markers, crayons
- A shoe box for each small group

Project

Throughout the author study, after each of the books about Peter is read, cooperative small groups should work together to discuss the different small moments that occurred in Peter's life. They can collect their ideas in a journal or on paper that they can refer to and add to as each of the four books is read and discussed. The students should reflect on their notes and ideas and create their own story about Peter, thinking of a new small moment that would be interesting to write about and share. They can create a scene in a shoebox, cutting out characters and setting details from construction paper and gluing them inside so it is easy for others to see what is happening. All cooperative small groups should have the opportunity to share their original "Peter" story and shoebox scene, explaining how and why they chose their small moment, how they decided on a setting, and how their story is similar to and different from the stories written by Ezra Jack Keats.

SHARED READING EXPERIENCE 4: EXPLORING CHARACTER TRAITS WITH JONATHAN LONDON

Author

Jonathan London

Grade-Level Recommendation

PreK–Grade 1

Books

- *Froggy Gets Dressed* (Puffin Books, 1994)
- *Froggy's First Kiss* (Puffin Books, 1999)
- *Froggy Goes to the Doctor* (Puffin Books, 2004)
- *Froggy Plays Soccer* (Puffin Books, 2001)

Materials

- Paper
- Writing supplies such as pencils and colored pencils
- Journals (optional)
- 1 poster board or large piece of chart paper for each group
- Art supplies such as construction paper, markers, and crayons

Project

Throughout the author study, after each of the books is read, cooperative small groups should work together to discuss the different characters in each story and the variety of character traits observed within each one. They can collect their ideas in a journal or on paper that they can refer to as each of the four books is read and discussed.

Each group should focus on a different character from the Froggy series and create a poster board or chart that displays the character's various personality traits. Teachers should model this by creating charts of characters from a book series that the class is familiar with. For example, if the class has already read *Corduroy* by Don Freeman (Puffin Books, 1976), the teacher might make a graphic organizer with a picture of Corduroy or Lisa with arrows and circles displaying the different personality traits of the characters chosen.

Teachers should assign different characters from the Froggy series to each cooperative work group. Students need to decide on the character traits together, citing evidence for the ones they choose to display. They should be encouraged to be creative with their project, using construction paper, markers, and crayons to represent the character and arrange the traits in an organized way. Each group should be given the opportunity to share their chart and explain their character to the whole class.

SHARED READING EXPERIENCE 5: WRITE DAVID SHANNON STYLE!

Author

David Shannon

Grade-Level Recommendation

PreK–Grade 1

Books

- *No, David!* (Blue Sky Press, 1998)
- *David Goes to School* (Blue Sky Press, 1999)
- *David Gets in Trouble* (Blue Sky Press, 2002)
- *It's Christmas, David!* (Blue Sky Press, 2010)

Materials

- Paper
- Writing supplies such as pencils, colored pencils
- Art supplies such as markers, crayons
- Two sheets of construction paper or card stock per group
- Stapler or hole punch and ribbon

Project

Throughout the author study, after each of the books is read, cooperative small groups should work together to discuss similarities in all the David Shannon books and how they are different from other books they have read or listened to. They should work together to create their own book in the style of David Shannon, featuring the main character, David. Each group should choose a different setting and create at least ten pages that can be bound with a construction paper or card stock cover.

When books have been finalized with either dictation from an adult for younger children or completed revisions for older children, they can be either stapled or tied together with a ribbon. It would be great for each group to have the opportunity to share their original book at a "David Shannon style" publishing party. Other classrooms in the school or families of the students could even be invited.

SHARED READING EXPERIENCE 6: FAVORITE E. B. WHITE FRIENDS IN THE NEWS

Author

E. B. White

Grade-Level Recommendation

Grades 1–3

Books

- *Charlotte's Web* (HarperCollins, 2012)
- *Stuart Little* (Harper and Row, 2005)
- *The Trumpet of the Swan* (HarperCollins, 2001)
- *A Boy, a Mouse, and a Spider: The Story of E. B. White* by Barbara Herkert (Henry Holt, 2017)

Materials

- Paper
- Writing supplies such as pencils and colored pencils
- Journals (optional)
- A variety of newspapers for inspiration

Project

Throughout the author study, after each of the books is read, cooperative small groups should work together to discuss and record their favorite animal fantasy scenes and events. They can collect their ideas in a journal or on paper that they can refer to as each of the books is read and discussed. Students should decide on three to five of their favorite scenes and write about them as if they were reporting the events in a newspaper. Each group will need to come up with their own newspaper title, headlines for each story, and pictures to accompany their writing. It would be helpful to share various actual newspapers with the class to guide and inspire students to make their projects as authentic as possible. Completed newspapers can be placed in the author study center or classroom library for all to read and enjoy.

SHARED READING EXPERIENCE 7: THE MOST INFLUENTIAL TEACHER

Author

Patricia Polacco

Grade-Level Recommendation

Grades 1–3

Books

- *Thank You, Mr. Falker* (Philomel Books, 2012)
- *The Junkyard Wonders* (Philomel Books, 2010)
- *An A from Miss Keller* (G. P Putnam's Sons Books for Young Readers, 2015)
- *The Art of Miss Chew* (G. P. Putnam's Sons Books for Young Readers, 2012)

Materials

- Paper
- Writing supplies such as pencils, colored pencils
- Art supplies such as crayons, markers, construction paper
- Journals (optional)
- Poster board or chart paper

Project

Throughout the author study, after each of the books is read, cooperative small groups should work together to discuss the teachers in each of the stories. They should record the influential words and actions of each of the teachers in a journal or on a paper that can be referred to and added to during the author study. It's important that students understand and make note of the actual things the teachers said and did that made them such great influences on the students involved. They need to decide together which one of the teachers was most influential and then create a persuasive poster and report highlighting the reasons why they chose that teacher. Each group should have the opportunity to present their persuasive essay and poster to the whole class.

SHARED READING EXPERIENCE 8: CELEBRATE KEVIN HENKES WITH STORY ELEMENT BLOCK TOWERS

Author

Kevin Henkes

Grade-Level Recommendation

Grades 1–3

Books

- *Lily's Purple Plastic Purse* (Greenwillow Books, 2006)
- *Chrysanthemum* (Mulberry Books, 2008)
- *Sheila Rae, the Brave* (Greenwillow Books, 1996)
- *Wemberly Worried* (Greenwillow Books, 2010)

Materials

- Paper
- Writing supplies such as pencils, colored pencils
- Journals (optional)
- 5 empty square tissue boxes for each small group
- Clear packing tape
- Art supplies (construction paper, crayons, markers, scissors, glue)

Project

Throughout the author study, after each of the books is read and discussed, cooperative small groups should work together to discuss the story elements within each one. Students should record the characters, setting, problem, and solution of each book in a journal or any paper that can be referred to and added to during the author study.

Each group should be assigned one of the stories to create a block tower that will display each of the elements. They will get five empty square tissue boxes to build their tower out of. The students can measure, cut, and glue construction paper to fit over each of the box sides, which they will then use to draw and write the story element details on. One of the boxes should be designed with the title and author, and that box should be at the top of the tower. The other boxes should have characters, setting, problem, and solution.

Cooperative groups can decide together how they are going to divide the work, but all the story element information should be discussed and decided on as a team. When all the blocks are complete, students need to assemble them into a tower. Packing tape works well for this. The story element block towers will make a great display in the classroom library or author study center once they have been shared and explained to the whole class.

SHARED READING EXPERIENCE 9: MAPPING WORLDS CREATED BY JON SCIESZKA

Author

Jon Scieszka

Grade-Level Recommendation

Grades 1–3

Books

- *The True Story of the Three Little Pigs* (Puffin Books, 1996)
- *The Stinky Cheese Man and Other Fairly Stupid Tales* (Viking Books for Young Readers, 1992)
- *The Frog Prince, Continued* (Puffin Books, 1994)
- *Battle Bunny* (Simon and Schuster Books for Young Readers, 2013)

Materials

- Paper
- Writing supplies such as pencils, colored pencils
- Journal (optional)
- Art supplies such as crayons, markers
- Butcher paper, large sheets of manila paper, chart paper
- Maps to use as samples and inspiration

Project

Throughout the author study, after each of the books is read and discussed, cooperative small groups should work together to discuss the settings and series of events that occurred in each story. Students should record this information in a journal or any paper that can be referred to and added to throughout the author study.

Students should also be exposed to many different maps. They should understand the purpose of maps and their common features. Students can work together to design a map to show the setting and chain of events that occurred in one of the four Jon Scieszka books studied. They should refer to the notes they collected during the author study and choose the book that is most interesting to the group. All teams should be given the time to share and discuss their map with the whole class. The maps would make a great display in the author study center or on a hallway bulletin board for the entire school to see!

SHARED READING EXPERIENCE 10: BEVERLY CLEARY CHARACTERS LIVE!

Author

Beverly Cleary

Grade-Level Recommendation

Grades 1–3

Books

- *Ramona the Pest* (HarperCollins, 2013)
- *Ramona and Her Father* (HarperCollins, 2013)
- *The Mouse and the Motorcycle* (HarperCollins, 2016)
- *Runaway Ralph* (HarperCollins, 2006)

Materials

- Paper
- Writing supplies such as pencils, colored pencils
- Journal (optional)
- Art supplies such as markers, crayons, scissors, glue

- A variety of recyclable materials, dress-up clothes, and props that can be used to create costumes, masks, and objects needed to perform a skit from each story

Project

Throughout the author study, after each of the books is read, cooperative small groups should work together to discuss and decide on what their favorite scenes are from each of the books. They should think about what it is specifically they like about them and create scripts in a reader's theater style so they can act them out. Students can record their scripts in a journal or any paper that can be referred to and added to throughout the author study. Once they have done this with their favorite scenes from each book, they need to choose one to practice and perform for the whole class. They can use art supplies, recyclable materials such as cardboard boxes and empty containers, and dress-up props to make their dramatization come to life for the class.

SHARED READING EXPERIENCE 11: FUDGE'S DIARY

Author

Judy Blume

Grade-Level Recommendation

Grades 4–6

Books

- *Tales of a Fourth Grade Nothing* (Puffin Books, 2007)
- *Superfudge* (Puffin Books, 2007)
- *Fudge-a-Mania* (Puffin Books, 2007)
- *Double Fudge* (Puffin Books, 2007)

Materials

- Paper
- Writing supplies such as pencils, colored pencils
- Journal (optional)

Project

Throughout the author study, after each of the books is read, cooperative small groups should work together to discuss and record what they believe are the thoughts and feelings of Fudge. They should write their ideas in a journal or any paper that can be referred to and added to throughout the author study. Once all the books are read and ideas are discussed and recorded, the groups should choose or be assigned one of the four books and imagine they are Fudge, writing a diary. They should write one diary entry for each chapter, and each group should have the opportunity to read all the entries to the class.

SHARED READING EXPERIENCE 12: DESIGNING FOR GORDON KORMAN

Author

Gordon Korman

Grade-Level Recommendation

Grades 4–6

Books

- *Ungifted* (Balzer and Bray, 2014)
- *Supergifted* (Balzer and Bray, 2018)
- *Swindle* (Scholastic, 2009)
- *The Unteachables* (Balzar & Bray, 2018)

Materials

- Paper
- Writing supplies such as pencils, colored pencils
- Journal (optional)
- Art supplies such as crayons, markers, construction paper

Project

Throughout the author study, after each of the books is read and discussed, cooperative small groups should work together to write a synopsis and discuss ideas for redesigning a cover for each book. They can record their work and thoughts in a journal or any paper that can be referred to and added to during the author study. Once all the books are read and discussed, each group should be assigned one of the books to create an original book cover. The book cover should show an important part of the story in the design and include a synopsis on the back. The book covers would make an excellent display in the author study center or classroom library.

SHARED READING EXPERIENCE 13: MISSING SCENES FROM FAVORITES BY DAHL

Author

Roald Dahl

Grade-Level Recommendation

Grades 4–6

Books

- *Charlie and the Chocolate Factory* (Puffin Books, 2007)
- *James and the Giant Peach* (Puffin Books, 2007)
- *Matilda* (Puffin Books, 2007)
- *The BFG* (Puffin Books, 2007)

Materials

- Paper
- Writing supplies such as pencils, colored pencils
- Art supplies such as construction paper, markers, crayons
- Journals (optional)

Project

Throughout the author study, after each of the books is read and discussed, cooperative small groups should work together to create scenes that are not in the book but would make sense if added. They can write their ideas in a journal or any paper that can be referred to or added to during the author study. Once all the books are read and discussed, teams can be assigned or choose one of the novels to focus on and add a "missing scene" to. They can create a mini book, telling where it would make sense within the Dahl novel, and should include several pages with detailed text and illustrations. All small groups should have the opportunity to share their "missing scene" book with the whole class.

SHARED READING EXPERIENCE 14: SEEING SPINELLI IN THE MOVIES

Author

Jerry Spinelli

Grade-Level Recommendation

Grades 4–6

Books

- *Maniac Magee* (Little, Brown Books for Young Readers, 1999)
- *Wringer* (HarperCollins, 2018)
- *Loser* (HarperCollins, 2018)
- *Eggs* (Little, Brown Books for Young Readers, 2008)

Materials

- Paper
- Writing supplies such as pencils, colored pencils
- Journal (optional)
- Art supplies such as markers, crayons
- Butcher paper, poster board, or chart paper

Project

Throughout the author study, after each of the books is read and discussed, cooperative small groups should work together to discuss how each book could be made into a movie. They should decide what actors and actresses should play the parts of the characters and how the movie could be advertised. They can record their ideas in a journal or any paper that can be referred to and added to during the author study.

Once all the books are read and discussed, teams should be assigned or choose one book that they will pretend is being made into a film and create an enticing movie poster for it as an advertisement. Posters should include each of the main characters from the novel with real actors and actresses listed. The advertisement should highlight the theme of the novel and state specific reasons to persuade people to see the movie. The posters should be shared and displayed in the author study center, classroom library, hallway, or even the school library.

SHARED READING EXPERIENCE 15: SUGGESTIONS FOR A WIMPY KID

Author

Jeff Kinney

Grade-Level Recommendation

Grades 4–6

Books

- *Diary of a Wimpy Kid* (Book 1) (Amulet Books, 2007)
- *The Ugly Truth* (Diary of a Wimpy Kid, Book 5) (Harry N. Abrams, 2010)
- *Cabin Fever* (Diary of a Wimpy Kid, Book 6) (Amulet Books, 2001)
- *Diary of a Wimpy Kid: The Getaway* (Harry N. Abrams, 2017)

Materials

- Paper
- Writing supplies such as pencils, colored pencils
- Journal (optional)
- Envelopes

Project

Throughout the author study, after each of the books is read, students should work together in their cooperative small groups to discuss the main character, Greg Heffley. They should record character traits, likes, dislikes, conflicts, and other details they notice about him, based on evidence from the text, in a journal or any paper they can refer to and add to during the author study.

Once all the books are read, teams should work together to write a letter to Greg Heffley. They should offer advice to help him solve his problems and also list suggestions for movies, songs, and books he might like. The letters should be realistic and helpful and should show evidence that the students have paid attention to Greg's characteristics. It would be great for teams to put their letters in real envelopes and exchange them with other teams to open and read together.

These experiences are meant to help build a community of readers, establish closer connections, improve communication skills, foster a love of books, and improve literacy skills during the early childhood and elementary years. Authentic learning will be inspired when students are engaged in these meaningful opportunities to discuss, extend, and respond creatively to wonderful literature by truly outstanding authors.

Books are a uniquely portable magic.

—Stephen King

Chapter Eight

Self-Expression through Innovative Art Integration

Fifteen Worthwhile Collaborative Projects to Inspire Creativity in Your Units of Study

Art washes away from the soul the dust of everyday life.
—Vincent Van Gogh

Students thrive on having opportunities to express themselves artistically. Art opens the door to creativity, critical thinking, and innovation. When teachers plan to integrate meaningful, expressive, and aesthetic activities to support the core curriculum, the impact is tremendous.

When students are also encouraged to work in a collaborative way, they learn to appreciate each other's contributions and unique skills. The collaborative art activities in this chapter will allow students to express themselves, contribute to the classroom in meaningful ways, and become more effective communicators. These projects are an awesome way to build community among students as they use their imaginations and have fun learning.

The collaborative art projects in this chapter are meant to be done with students arranged in small groups of three to five. There should be a whole-group introduction to each activity, time for students to collaborate and create, and time for the whole class to meet again to share and debrief. Cooperative group work expectations should be established and posted so they are easily seen and understood by all students and could include the following:

- Get along.

- Respect others.
- Stay on task.
- Use quiet voices.
- Participate.
- Stay in your group.

COLLABORATIVE ART PROJECT 1: STARS AND STRIPES MOSAIC ART

Subject/Content

Social studies/U.S. history: Betsy Ross

Literature Suggestions

- PreK–Grade 2: *Easy Reader Biographies: Betsy Ross: The Story of Our Flag* by Pamela Chanko (Scholastic Teaching Resources, 2007)
- Grades 3–6: *Betsy Ross and the Flag* (Landmark Books #26) by Jane (Rothschild) Mayer (Random House, 1952)

Materials

- Red, white, and blue construction paper
- Scissors and glue
- U.S. flag
- Betsy Ross flag (picture or replica)
- Large poster board or sheet of chart paper with the U.S. flag drawn with black permanent marker

Process

Teachers can begin by reading one of the suggested titles or a similar book to introduce students to the Betsy Ross flag and U.S. flag. Students should then work in cooperative groups to discuss similarities and differences in the flags. They will work together to make their own "mosaic" or "tear art" flag by tearing pieces of red, white, and blue construction paper into small pieces and gluing them on the premade flag outline. Each group should share their mosaic flag creation with the whole class and discuss successes and challenges that they experienced while creating as a team.

COLLABORATIVE ART PROJECT 2: BRANCHES OF GOVERNMENT

Subject/Content

Social studies/U.S. history: democracy

Literature Suggestions

- PreK–Grade 2: *A More Perfect Union: The Story of Our Constitution* by Betsy Maestro (HarperCollins, 2008)
- Grades 3–6: *Our Government: The Three Branches* (Social Studies Readers: Content and Literacy) by Shelly Buchanan (Teacher Created Materials, 2014)

Materials

- Construction paper
- Butcher paper or brown paper bags
- Poster board
- Markers
- Glue
- Scissors

Process

Students will first need to understand the concept of democracy and how it works. Teachers can support this by choosing, reading, and discussing one of the above-listed books or similar for their students' level. Teachers and students should work together to create an anchor chart that clearly explains the three branches of government and their responsibilities. Students will then work in their collaborative groups to create a picture of a tree with branches representing the three branches of government (judicial, executive, legislative) and leaves showing the responsibilities of each branch (enforces laws, makes policies and budgets, makes laws, etc.).

Students should be encouraged to be as creative as possible when designing their trees. They can use the brown bags or butcher paper to make a three-dimensional model or a mural type of representation. Once students have had the time to plan, create, and reflect, they should have the opportunity to present and display their project to the whole class. It's important for students to discuss what they learned and successes and challenges they experienced while creating as a team.

COLLABORATIVE ART PROJECT 3: COLORFUL CITYSCAPES

Subject/Content

Social studies/city neighborhoods

Literature Suggestions

- PreK–Grade 2: *The Snowy Day* by Ezra Jack Keats (Puffin Books, 1976)
- Grades 3–6: *A Chair for My Mother* by Vera B. Williams (Greenwillow Books, 2007)

Materials

- Books with various pictures of apartment buildings
- 2-inch-wide paintbrushes
- Watercolors
- Art paper
- Pencils
- Permanent fine-tipped marking pens

Process

To prepare for this cooperative art activity, teachers should display pictures of apartment buildings. There are also many children's books to share, such as the above-suggested titles, that show city scenes in artistic ways. Teachers should take time with the whole group to discuss architecture, including the different kinds of doors, windows, and porches that are shown in the books. Students can then work in their small cooperative groups to create watercolor murals of a city neighborhood. They can be shown the technique of first using watercolors, allowing them to dry, and then adding details with permanent markers.

Teachers should encourage the students to be creative, share ideas, and communicate respectfully while groups are working to complete their mural. All groups should have the opportunity to present and discuss their original creations with the class, mentioning successes and challenges they experienced.

COLLABORATIVE ART PROJECT 4: RAIN REPRESENTATIONS

Subject/Content

Science/weather

Literature Suggestions

- PreK–Grade 2: *Rain* (Seasons with Granddad) by Sam Usher (Templar, 2017)
- Grades 3–6: *Hurricane* by David Wiesner (Clarion Books, 1992)

Materials

- Construction paper
- Colored pencils
- Markers
- White colored pencil
- Chalk
- Plastic knives, plastic pizza cutters, and other common tools that may create artistic effects

Process

Teachers should begin this activity by sharing illustrations of rain blowing across windows (such as in suggested books). Students can then work cooperatively to think of ways they can create the same effects, such as creating rain by slashing their colored pictures with the knives, chalk edges, or white colored pencils. Teachers should encourage students to experiment with different techniques. It's important that groups have a sufficient amount of time to create several weather pictures and rain representations so they can explore alternate ways of creating the same effects. All groups should have the opportunity to present their ideas and methods to the class, mentioning successes and challenges they experienced.

COLLABORATIVE ART PROJECT 5: PUEBLO ARCHITECTURE

Subject/Content

Social studies/Native American culture

Literature Suggestions

- PreK–Grade 2: *Arrow to the Sun* by Gerald McDermott (Puffin Books, 1977)
- Grades 3–6: *The Pueblo* (True Books) by Kevin Cunningham (Children's Press, 2011)

Materials

- Homemade Pueblo clay ingredients (1 cup sand, 1/2 cup cornstarch, 3/4 cup liquid starch, 1 tablespoon powdered tempera paint)
- Hot plate
- Pan
- Heat-resistant mixing spoon
- Paint and paintbrushes or permanent markers
- Pictures of Pueblo villages, books suggested above, or similar

Process

Teachers may choose to prepare this clay ahead of time or invite students to prepare it with them as part of a center rotation. It's very easy to prepare by simply combining sand and cornstarch in a pan, adding liquid starch and powdered paint, and cooking over medium heat on a stove or hot plate. The mixture will thicken and turn into dough. Once it cools, it only needs to be kneaded for twenty to thirty seconds before using. The sculptures created will stay permanently hard when dry.

Once the clay is ready to be used, students should work in their collaborative groups to plan and create Native American villages inspired by Pueblo Indian culture. They should have access to pictures of Pueblo dwellings and literature (such as suggested titles above) that present authentic representations and reliable information about this southwest tribe, which has flourished for thousands of years.

All cooperative work groups should have the opportunity to share their Pueblo designs with the whole class and discuss successes and challenges they experienced while learning and creating.

COLLABORATIVE ART PROJECT 6: TEAM TOTEM POLE

Subject/Content

Social studies/Native American culture

Literature Suggestions

- PreK–Grade 2: *Totem Tale: A Tall Story from Alaska* by Deb Vanasse (Little Bigfoot, 2006)
- Grades 3–6: *North American Totem Poles: Secrets and Symbols of North America* by Molly Perham (Firefly Books, 1999)

Materials

- Recycled cylindrical containers, such as oatmeal or coffee cans
- Construction paper
- Scissors
- Markers, crayons, or paint and paintbrushes
- Tape
- Pictures of authentic Native American totem poles or literature such as titles suggested above

Process

Teachers can begin this collaborative art project by showing students pictures and reading books (such as the titles suggested above) about Native American totem poles. Each member of each group should have his or her own cylindrical container. Each group needs to tape its containers together, one on top of the other. Next, each group needs to wrap colorful construction paper around the cans, being sure to tape it down securely.

Once each group has their totem pole secure and covered, each member of the group needs to decorate an equal portion of the totem pole in a meaningful and creative way. The team will need to cut equal pieces of plain paper for each member of the group. Each member will think of an important event in his or her life and make a design that stands for the event. Once each member of the team has created his or her design and attached it to the totem pole, group members can present it to the class, explaining the meaning of each design and also discussing successes and challenges their group experienced while designing their team totem poles.

COLLABORATIVE ART PROJECT 7: HIDDEN JUNGLE BIRD DIORAMA

Subject/Content

Science/jungle bird camouflage

Literature Suggestions

- PreK–Grade 2: *One Day in the Tropical Rainforest* by Jean Craighead George (HarperCollins, 1995)
- Grades 3–6: *A Walk in the Rainforest* (Biomes of North America) by Rebecca L. Johnson (Lerner Classroom, 2001)

Materials

- 1 large box for each cooperative group
- 1 empty toilet tissue or paper towel roll for each student
- Brown paint, various colorful shades of paint, and paintbrushes
- Green tissue paper
- Blank paper
- Scissors
- Glue
- Tape

Process

This activity is a perfect integration for the study of bird defenses. Teachers should prepare for this collaborative art project by teaching students about camouflage (when an animal's body covering looks similar to the surroundings that the animal lives in and the animal uses this as a natural defense mechanism) and about the types of jungle birds that use camouflage to survive.

Each cooperative group should have one box to turn into a camouflaged jungle bird diorama scene. Each member of the group needs to create a bird out of blank paper. The birds for each group need to be the same color that the entire group decides on. The students should also decide together what color to paint the inside of their box. They should create an interior that will help the birds hide.

Once the birds and background are complete, the students need to create trees by painting the toilet or paper towel tubes brown and adding green tissue paper for leaves. Once all pieces are dry and assembled into original hidden bird scenes, students should reflect on their work and group experience. Each cooperative work group should be given the opportunity to share their diorama with the entire class, mentioning successes and challenges they experienced throughout the creative process.

COLLABORATIVE ART PROJECT 8: MASTERPIECE STORYTELLING

Subject/Content

Fine arts/speaking and listening, storytelling

Literature Suggestions

- PreK–Grade 2 and Grades 3–6: *I Like Art: Renaissance* and *I Like Art: Expressionism* both by Margaux Stanitsas (Xist, 2018)
- Grades 3–6: *Spot the Differences Book 3: Art Masterpiece Mysteries* by Dover (Dover Children's Activity Books, 2012)

Materials

- Reproductions of paintings or books such as suggested titles above that contain many examples of artistic masterpieces
- Paper and writing supplies

Process

Each small cooperative work group will be given a work of art to carefully study. The groups should be allowed time to carefully inspect the art and take notes on the different qualities they notice that are meaningful to them. All members of the group need to pay attention to, and explain, how the painting makes them feel, what it reminds them of, and overall, what it means to them. They will then work together to combine their interpretations into one story, which should be written down and shared with the whole class.

COLLABORATIVE ART PROJECT 9: HEALTHY FOOD FINGERPRINT DOODLES

Subject/Content

Health/nutrition

Literature Suggestions

- PreK–Grade 2: *Gregory the Terrible Eater* by Mitchell Sharmat (Scholastic, 2009)
- Grades 3–6: *Chocolate Fever* by Robert Kimmel Smith (Puffin Books, 2006)

Materials

- Ink pads
- Permanent markers
- 1 poster board or chart paper per group

Process

This project is best completed after students have been taught about healthy food choices. The students will work together to first brainstorm a balanced list of healthy foods. Once they have come up with several different ideas, they can then decide together how they can best represent them on their poster board or chart paper by only using their fingerprints, inkpads, and permanent markers.

Teachers should encourage students to be creative, to communicate with each other, and to experiment with the limited amount of materials to make unique representations of healthy food choices for their team poster. All groups should have the opportunity to present their projects to the class, sharing successes and challenges experienced during brainstorming and creating. The posters would be wonderful to display in a health room or cafeteria.

COLLABORATIVE ART PROJECT 10: PUERTO RICAN CARNIVAL MASKS

Subject/Content

Social studies/multicultural awareness

Literature Suggestions

- PreK–Grade 2: *Rafi and Rosi Carnival!* (Dive into Reading) by Lulu Delacre (Children's Book Press, 2016)
- Grades 3–6: *Puerto Rico* by Deborah Kent (Children's Press, 1991)

Materials

- Paper plates
- Craft sticks
- Liquid starch
- Tempera paint in bright colors
- Paintbrushes
- Brightly colored tissue paper
- Tape
- Pictures of Puerto Rican Carnival masks

Process

This project will enrich a study of Puerto Rican life in the United States by allowing students to reenact the traditional Puerto Rican Carnival in a hands-on, creative, and cooperative way. Before beginning this project, students should be taught about the daily life and customs of Puerto Ricans, especially about Carnival, which is a time of parades and feasting before Lent.

Teachers should begin this project by finding pictures of Carnival masks (suggested literature selections above have many) to share with students. They can then have students work in their cooperative groups to create their own. Each group will decide together how they will create masks that have the same common elements as traditional Puerto Rican Carnival masks, have some sort of common theme within the small group, and also have individual details within each one, allowing for self-expression and individuality.

The first step in creating the masks is to prepare the tissue paper. This can be easily done by students when they use a spatter paint technique on the tissue paper. They can do this by dipping a paintbrush in paint (a very small amount) and shaking it all over the paper. Students should use contrasting colors to achieve a design similar to traditional Puerto Rican Carnival masks. Once the paint is dry, the tissue paper can be cut into six-by-six-inch squares.

The students need to brush starch on a paper plate. They can then cover the plate with the squares of tissue paper. When plates are dry, the students can trim the edges of the tissue paper. They need to draw eyes and a mouth on their paper plates and cut them out. Other details, such as cutting out a nose and ears and/or horns from construction paper and gluing them to the mask, can be added, and then students should tape a craft stick to the base of the masks to make them functional.

Once every team has their Puerto Rican Carnival masks ready, they should be given the opportunity to wear their masks and present their creations to the class. They might choose to research and perform a Puerto Rican dance or reenact a parade that might occur during Carnival time. Each group should also discuss successes and challenges their group experienced throughout the process of planning and creating.

COLLABORATIVE ART PROJECT 11: COLLECTIVE NOUN CELEBRATIONS

Subject/Content

English and language arts/vocabulary study

Literature Suggestions

- PreK–Grade 2: *A Cache of Jewels and Other Collective Nouns* by Ruth Heller (Puffin Books, 1998)
- Grades 3–6: *A Compendium of Collective Nouns: From an Armory of Aardvarks to a Zeal of Zebras* by Woop Studios (Chronicle Books, 2013)

Materials

- Variety of art supplies such as paints, brushes, markers, pastels, crayons, colored pencils
- Paper
- Scissors
- Tape or glue
- Stapler and staples

Process

Students should first have several opportunities to learn about and explore collective nouns. The literature selections above have beautiful illustrations

Self-Expression through Innovative Art Integration 139

and extend the vocabulary in artistic and imaginative ways. Students should use the text appropriate for their level to inspire them to come up with their own ideas for other collective nouns to illustrate.

Each cooperative group will create their own book of collective nouns with original pictures and artwork. They will decide together how to best accomplish this and should be encouraged to experiment with different art materials and explore different ways to structure their book. All groups should have the opportunity to share their books with the whole class, discussing successes and challenges experienced during the creative process. Original collective noun books are a wonderful addition to a classroom library or writing center.

COLLABORATIVE ART PROJECT 12: RECYCLED FLOWER GARDEN

Literature Suggestions

- PreK–Grade 2: *Planting a Rainbow* by Lois Ehlert (HMH Books for Young Readers, 2003)
- Grades 3–6: *The Kids' Guide to Exploring Nature* (BBG Guides for a Greener Planet) by Brooklyn Botanic Garden Educators (Brooklyn Botanic Garden, 2015)

Materials

- Recycled paper and cardboard collected from classroom and home over the course of several days
- Scissors
- Glue
- Colored pencils or crayons

Process

Students and teachers can prepare for this art project by collecting paper scraps (trash) from both the classroom and home. They also need to research different types of flowers. The literature suggestions above are great introductions to the world of botany and have many examples of different varieties of flowers to share with students.

Once the paper scraps are collected and students have been exposed to different types of flowers, they can work cooperatively to plan and create their own team flower garden using only recycled paper and cardboard. Students can plan their garden by sketching flowers on paper with colored pencils or crayons, but the actual garden must be created solely with paper scraps, cardboard, scissors, and glue.

All groups should have the opportunity to share their team flower gardens with the whole class, discussing successes and challenges their group experienced throughout the creative process. The team gardens may also be brought together as a beautiful classroom display. This would be a perfect Earth Day project and a great way to brighten up the hallways of an entire school.

COLLABORATIVE ART PROJECT 13: BUTTERFLY LIFE CYCLE CREATION

Subject/Content

Science/life process of a butterfly

Literature Suggestions

- PreK–Grade 2: *Monarch Butterfly* by Gail Gibbons (Holiday House, 1989)
- Grades 3–6: *The Monarch: Saving Our Most-Loved Butterfly* by Kylee Baumle (St. Lynn's Press, 2017)
- For all ages: *The Life Cycles of Butterflies: From Egg to Maturity, a Visual Guide to 23 Common Garden Butterflies* by Judy Burris (Storey, 2006)

Materials

- Construction paper
- Variety of collage art supplies such as buttons, pasta, pom-poms, and pipe cleaners
- Paper plates
- Scissors
- Glue
- Markers, colored pencils, or crayons
- Small twigs
- Play dough or clay
- Googly eyes

Process

This project is a fantastic way for students to work together to re-create what they have learned about the stages of a butterfly life cycle. The suggested literature above explains the process beautifully. Students can use the texts appropriate for their grade level for research and clarification as they plan a way to use the art materials to make their own team model of the butterfly life cycle, showing each stage of a butterfly's life.

    The paper plate may be used as a structured canvas for each group's model. It would be great if it was separated in four sections, with students using a section for each stage (egg, caterpillar, pupa, adult), but all students should be encouraged to work within their group to be creative and original as they choose their own way to accurately show the stages of the butterfly life cycle. All cooperative groups should have the opportunity to share and explain their work, discussing successes and challenges experienced while planning and creating their model.

COLLABORATIVE ART PROJECT 14:
KINDNESS QUOTE ARTISTIC RESPONSE

Subject/Content

Social studies/social emotional awareness

Literature Suggestions

- PreK–Grade 2: *We're All Wonders* by R. J. Palacio (Knopf Books for Young Readers, 2017)
- Grades 3–6: *Wonder* by R. J. Palacio (Knopf Books for Young Readers, 2012)

Materials

- Various collage art supplies such as yarn, tissue paper squares, pasta pieces, buttons, fabric swatches
- Construction paper
- Poster board
- Markers, colored pencils, or crayons
- Scissors
- Glue

Process

Students should be explicitly taught the importance of kindness and choices they can make to make others feel good about themselves. There are several wonderful books that do a beautiful job expressing this message, such as the literature suggestions above. Teachers need to choose a kindness quote or have students come up with their own to respond to in an artistic way.

One popular quote for this project is "If you see someone without a smile, give them one of yours," from Dolly Parton. Students can be very creative when showing ways to "give" someone a smile! There are also many great quotes from Kid President, such as, "Be somebody that makes everybody feel like a somebody," "Create something that will make the world more awesome," and "Throw kindness around like confetti!"

Students should be given the time and opportunity to discuss their given quote or choose a quote of their own. They should decide as a team how they are going to represent the quote in an artistic way. Once all cooperative groups plan and create their projects, they should be shared with the whole class and displayed to serve as kindness reminders to all.

COLLABORATIVE ART PROJECT 15: POINTILLISM SOLAR SYSTEM

Subject/Content

Science/solar system

Literature Suggestions

- PreK–Grade 2: *The Magic School Bus Lost in the Solar System* by Joanna Cole (Scholastic, 1992)
- Grades 3–6: *Space: A Visual Encyclopedia* by DK (DK Children, 2010)

Materials

- Paper
- Pencils
- Q-tips
- Paint

Process

Pointillism is an art technique where pictures are created using dots of ink or paint. Students will love experimenting with this method of art by using Q-tips and paint and creating a representation of a topic they have studied. Teachers who have introduced their class to the solar system will find the above-suggested books to be excellent resources in further teaching and preparing students for this project.

Students should be instructed to work in cooperative groups to plan and create an artistic representation of the solar system using pointillism. Teachers can show the students how to achieve the pointillism effect by instructing them to first sketch the pictures they need and then color them in with dots of paint using Q-tips. All groups should have the opportunity to share their pointillism solar system projects with the whole class, discussing successes and challenges they experienced while planning and creating.

The possibilities are endless when it comes to using the pointillism method for art integration. Other units of study that lend themselves well to this technique are the four seasons, cultural studies, and animal classifications. It's amazing how students can use simple materials such as Q-tips and paint, their imaginations, and the input of each other to create true masterpieces based on important academic topics!

SUMMARY

When teachers take the time to provide innovative experiences such as these, integrating art with important units of study, students benefit in many ways. Visual arts teach them about color, layout, perspective, and balance. These are all important concepts that are necessary for students to understand when presenting academic work in school and later in their career of choice.

Having opportunities to be purposefully creative helps students to develop problem-solving skills, motor skills, language skills, and social skills. It also allows them to take risks and be inventive. Integrating the arts with other subject matter reaches students who might not be otherwise engaged in class assignments. When students are allowed to express themselves artistically, they are taught to take their time to be more careful and observant in how they view and interpret the world.

The arts connect students with their own culture as well as with the wider world and challenges learners at all levels. Art helps students be more like their true selves rather than like everyone else.

Art is as natural as sunshine and as vital as nourishment.
—MaryAnn F. Kohl

Chapter Nine

Let Them Move!

Fifteen Ways to Improve Physical Fitness, Support Academic Concepts, and Increase Authentic Learning

> *Physical fitness is not only one of the most important keys to a healthy body, it is the basis of dynamic and creative intellectual activity.*
> —John F. Kennedy

A surefire way to inspire and increase authentic student learning, enhance concentration, boost on-task behavior, and improve student attitudes is to add movement in the classroom. An amazing thing about movement is that it also decreases stress levels while increasing happiness levels!

Teachers can make sure students get the movement they need by integrating movement into lessons, using cooperative learning activities, and adding brain breaks throughout the day. The activities in this chapter will keep students moving each day in meaningful ways.

All teachers know that students naturally need to move, and when movement is incorporated purposefully, distracting movements decrease. Children are able to focus better, collaborate more effectively, and unlock their imaginations in productive ways.

It's exciting when teachers can integrate physical activity into meaningful and enjoyable lessons. The students become highly engaged, and authentic learning is enhanced.

MOVEMENT ACTIVITY 1: IMPROVISED STORY DRAMATIZATION

Materials

- An action-packed book suitable for the grade level of students taught
- Chart paper
- Markers

Book Suggestions

Grades: PreK and K

- *The Three Billy Goats Gruff* by Paul Galdone (HMH Books for Young Readers, 1981)
- *Caps for Sale* by Esphyr Slobodkina (HarperCollins, 1987)
- *Millions of Cats* by Wanda Gag (Puffin Books, 2006)

Grades 1 and 2

- *Hurricane Heroes in Texas* (Magic Tree House) by Mary Pope Osborne (Random House, 2018)
- *Where the Wild Things Are* by Maurice Sendak (HarperCollins, 1984)
- *Arrow to the Sun* by Gerald McDermott (Puffin Books, 1977)

Grades 3 and 4

- *The Mouse and the Motorcycle* by Beverly Cleary (HarperCollins, 2016)
- *Charlotte's Web* by E. B. White (HarperCollins, 2012)
- *Mufaro's Beautiful Daughters: An African Tale* by John Steptoe (Puffin Books, 2008)

Grades 5 and 6

- *How to Train Your Dragon: How to Be a Pirate* by Cressida Cowell (Little, Brown Books for Young Readers, 2010)
- *Swindle* by Gordon Korman (Scholastic, 2009)
- *Founding Mothers* by Cokie Roberts (HarperCollins, 2014)

Skills

- Reading comprehension
- Language development

- Arts standards (drama)
- Variety of locomotor and nonlocomotor skills

Strategy

One of the most fulfilling ways to enjoy a great story is to extend it by dramatizing it. Improvised story dramatization has positive effects on both language development and reading comprehension for students in pre-K all the way through middle school.

Choose a book to dramatize that is grade-level appropriate and may be related to other content areas of study in your classroom. To maximize the physical activity, be sure the book is action packed and has many opportunities for movement.

Younger students love to dramatize picture books that have repeated phrases to chant. Older students benefit from traditional literature, such as folktales and myths and legends, which may be related to what they are studying in American history, the history and traditions of world cultures, or the ancient world.

Ideally, the stories will have a clear story line, strong characters, repeated dialogue, and importantly, a character or element that many students can play at the same time so that all students will be up, moving, and involved in each dramatization.

Procedure

- Reread and discuss the story. Teachers of younger students can repeatedly read aloud and older students can read and discuss the story in small groups. Students should be asked to pay attention to the setting, characters, and sequence of events or plot as well as the most exciting parts, the mood and theme, and things characters say.
- Make a story chart. Teachers of younger students can record students' ideas about each story element on chart paper to prepare for the dramatization. Older students can do this in groups.
- Create a map of the classroom. It is important to use the entire space, adjust furniture as needed, and add settings needed for the story. The sequence of events should be numbered, and arrows are needed to show the direction of the flow of action.
- Do a walkthrough. Teachers can ask for volunteers to act out the story for the first time, but all students should be engaged in this step, either by playing kinds of characters that can be played by many students or as an active audience.

- Debrief and discuss the positive parts of the improvised story dramatization. Teachers should encourage students to decide on specific things to do to improve the play.
- Act it out again, implementing the planned improvements.

MOVEMENT ACTIVITY 2: MATH CONCEPT GALLERY WALK

Materials

- Index cards
- Card stock
- Laminated paper or paper placed in dry-erase pockets (anything that can be used to write tasks on and be posted in various areas of the classroom)
- A teacher- or student-created recording sheet and clipboard
- Notebook (optional)

Skills

- Mathematical skills and concepts for every topic and level
- Variety of locomotor and nonlocomotor skills

Strategy

A gallery walk is a fantastic way to integrate movement into a math lesson. During a gallery walk, cards are posted around the room, each containing a task for students to complete. Students move all around the room, completing their tasks on their recording sheet.

A gallery walk is a wonderful way to cater to the needs of your students because you can create any task you feel will help the students master a particular skill. Teachers often have students working on different topics and at different levels, so they color code their task cards. For example, one group might be asked to complete their gallery walk by searching for all red task cards and another group will search for the appropriately differentiated blue cards.

Task Card Examples

PreK and K

- Find three items that are yellow. Find two items that are red. How many items do you have now? Show your work on your recording sheet.

- How many blocks would it take to measure your foot? How many blocks would it take to measure your friend's foot? Whose foot is longer? How do you know? Show your work on the recording sheet.

Grades 1 and 2

- Skip count by tens. What are the missing numbers? 545, ___, 565, ___, 585. Show your work on the recording sheet.
- Write the correct value. Starting number: 260
- What is one more? ___ What is one less? ___ What is ten more? ___ What is one hundred more? ___ What is one hundred less? ___
- Write your answers on the recording sheet.

Grades 3 and 4

- Write a story problem on your recording sheet for this equation. 5x6=30
- Look at the addition problems below. For each one, write a multiplication equation on your recording sheet that could be used as a shortcut.

    1. 3+3+3=9
    2. 5+5+5+5=20
    3. 2+2+2+2+2=10

Grades 5 and 6

- The students at Kennedy Elementary School are going on a field trip to the Museum of Fine Arts. Two thousand thirty-eight students are going on Tuesday, and 1,456 are going on Wednesday. Mr. West, the principal, wants to order special school name tags that come in packs of five hundred. Each package costs $9.25.

    1. How many packages does Mr. West need to order?
    2. How much will the packages cost?

- David has forty-five minutes left before the concert ends. It is 10:05 p.m. What time does the concert end?

Teachers set up for their gallery walk by creating task cards suitable to their students' skill and level. Index cards, card stock, and laminated colored paper are all popular choices; however, vinyl dry-erase pockets work well too because they can be kept on the wall and only the paper or card inside needs to change.

An effective gallery walk will have the task cards mounted on walls, bookshelves, file cabinets, and so on. They should be spaced so that no two are too close together. Students can use clipboards with recording sheets and pencils attached. Some teachers have their students keep a gallery walk notebook as an alternative to clipboards and recording sheets. Whichever way it's done, it's always a fantastic way to get students moving while they're learning!

MOVEMENT ACTIVITIES 3–7: HOLIDAYS AROUND THE WORLD INTEGRATION

Materials

- Construction paper
- Craft supplies such as paper plates, pie tins, oatmeal containers, dried beans, and yarn to make instruments and a faux snowball and a wreath

Skills

- Multicultural awareness
- Cooperation
- Variety of locomotor and nonlocomotor skills

Strategy

There are so many unique and wonderful dances, sports, and games in every culture. Teaching students about multicultural holidays, customs, and festivals around the globe provides excellent opportunities to integrate movement into any classroom.

Activity 3: Los Posadas Game

During Christmas in Mexico, children play the game Las Posadas. When engaging students in this game, encourage players to take turns being the leader of the group. Four or five other players will be the innkeepers. The innkeepers need to gather together and decide which one will be the innkeeper who says "yes" without letting the leader know who it is. The innkeepers then stand in a circle facing out. The rest of the students follow the leader as he or she pretends to knock at the innkeeper's door, asking, "May Mary rest here?" When the group gets to the innkeeper who says "yes," all the students should cheer and follow the innkeeper around the classroom (or playground) singing the holiday song of his or her choice.

Activity 4: Christmas Parade Down Under

In Australia, Christmas comes in the summer. Families have picnics at the beach or in the country. They gather to watch marching parades and marching bands. Students will love pretending to be in Australia by putting on a parade with marching bands and floats. Floats can easily be designed by students on large pieces of construction paper that they may attach to their clothing with a clip. Students are enthusiastic about creating elaborate floats based on research about Australia. Other students can form the marching band, putting bathing suits and other warm weather attire over their clothing to add to the summery Australian Christmas spirit.

Activity 5: Indian Rhythm

On Christmas Day, Christian Indians wear their brightest clothes to church. During the church service, they sing and play a variety of musical instruments, including drums, cymbals, and tambourines. Students can make their own instruments, such as pie tin cymbals, oatmeal container drums, and paper plate/dried bean tambourines and then dance and sing along to traditional carols.

Activity 6: The Festival of Light

The Christmas season begins each year in Sweden on St. Lucia Day, December 13. The day honors St. Lucia, who lived in Italy during the fourth century. At that time Christians were not allowed to practice their religion, and many Christians hid in tunnels so they could continue to pray. Lucia carried food into the tunnels to help the Christians. Because the tunnels were dark, she wore a crown made out of evergreen with candles attached to it so she could find her way to bring the Christians food.

St. Lucia Day is also called the Festival of Light. The day is said to bring brightness and hope to the people of Sweden during the darkest time of the year. Students will enjoy playing the game Wreath Ball as they learn about St. Lucia and the Festival of Light. Teachers or students can make a "snow" ball from yarn, papier-mâché, or fabric and pillow stuffing. Teachers can then suspend a sturdy wreath from the ceiling or a tree branch if they choose to play outside. Students will enjoy taking turns trying to throw the snowball through the wreath. It can be made more challenging depending on how far away the students stand and could also be played in teams as a relay event.

Activity 7: Christmas in Norway

Norwegians believed a long time ago that witches and evil spirits came out on Christmas Eve. This superstition brought about the tradition of hiding brooms and fireplace utensils. On Christmas Eve, Norwegians hide all the brooms in the house to keep the witches from riding them. Fire shovels and tongs are hidden from spirits too. Some Norwegians still follow these traditions.

Students will have fun playing the Norwegian-inspired game Hide the Broom. Teachers can use a small whisk broom or cut a miniature broom from construction paper. Students can take turns being "it." The child who is "it" needs to cover his or her eyes. Another student needs to be the "hider." The rest of the class needs to watch as the hider finds a place for the broom. When the broom is hidden, tell "it" to begin searching for the broom. As "it" gets closer to the broom, the students tap on their desks, getting louder and faster as he or she gets closer and quieter and slower as he or she gets farther from the hiding place. When "it" finds the broom, two more players can play the parts of "it" and "hider."

MOVEMENT ACTIVITIES 8–11: NATIVE AMERICAN INTEGRATION

Materials

- 6 jump ropes
- 6 hula hoops
- 3 beanbags
- 12 small stuffed animals
- 15 cones
- 22 whiffle balls
- 3 cups
- 3 scoops
- 6 empty baskets
- 3 baskets of a dozen tennis balls
- 36 manipulatives

Skills

- Historical, physical geography, and climate awareness
- Cooperation
- A variety of locomotor and nonlocomotor skills

Strategy

Teaching students about how physical geography and climate influenced the ways in which Native American tribes lived provides great opportunities for

movement integration for students at every grade level. These activities will allow students to better understand how the Native Americans survived the four seasons as they perform physical activities to reenact what took place long ago. These four activities can be done together as students rotate in small groups from movement activity to movement activity, or they can be done as part of a center rotation involving other subjects and skills.

For example, one group of students might be reading about Native Americans in the winter, while another group could be writing an informational piece about Native American life. Teachers know that students need a variety of opportunities to learn, process, and extend information and might even have a Native American art center involving weaving, pottery, and sand painting or a cooking center with directions and ingredients required to make a Native American–inspired recipe.

Activity 8: Native Americans in the Winter (Hunting)

Teachers can easily set up this activity by placing three hula hoops with four stuffed animals in each on the ground. They can then place cones and beanbags a few feet (up to ten feet for older students) away from each hoop. Students will toss the beanbag into the hoop to capture an animal for their group. If they miss, they take the beanbag back to the cone and try again. If they do manage to capture an animal, they will run to collect the animal and bring it back to the cone. Students can continue to attempt to capture the animals until time is up or all four animals are captured.

Activity 9: Native Americans in the Spring (Berry Picking and Fishing)

Students will complete this activity in two parts. The first part is set up by placing the buckets of balls (berries) about three to ten feet (depending on age and ability of students) away from the empty buckets and three starting cones. The students will run back and forth from the empty bucket to the full bucket (berry bush), get a ball (berry), and bring it back. They continue until all "berries" are picked.

The second part will require three buckets (fishing holes) one to five feet (depending on age and skill level of students) away from beginning cones with six jump ropes (fishing rods) at each cone. Students have to try to underhand flip the jump rope into the bucket. If the handle lands in the bucket, they have caught a fish.

Activity 10: Native Americans in the Summer (Planting)

Start by setting up three cones as starting spots. Each cone needs to have a cup with twelve manipulatives (seeds). The students pick one seed out of the cup at a time and put it in an assigned spot. The students continue to go back and forth to the cup to get another "seed" to plant until they are all planted directly in a row in front of them. There should be three rows of planted "seeds" at the end.

Activity 11: Native Americans in the Fall (Harvest)

Teachers can place three cones to act as starting lines and add a scoop to each one. Six to eight whiffle balls can be lined up directly in front of each starting cone to resemble crops that need to be harvested. A hoop should be placed behind each starting cone to represent the collecting basket. Students at each cone will love running out to try to scoop up one whiffle ball (crops) and return to place it in the basket. They can continue until all crops have been picked.

MOVEMENT ACTIVITY 12:
INSECT DEFENSE SCIENCE INTEGRATION

Materials

- Music
- Chart paper
- Markers

Suggested Books

- *The Illustrated World Encyclopedia of Insects* by Martin Walters (Lorenz Books, 2011)
- *Animal Defenses: How Animals Protect Themselves* by Etta Kaner (Kids Can Press, 1999)
- *How Do Insects Protect Themselves?* (Insects Close-Up) by Megan Kopp (Crabtree, 2015)

Skills

- Awareness of insect defense mechanisms
- Cooperation
- A variety of locomotor and nonlocomotor skills

Strategy

Teachers and students will work together to research different insect defenses, such as their abilities to camouflage, sting, and escape. They will then practice their new knowledge by dramatizing the different insects and mechanisms they use. Research can be completed by searching through grade-appropriate nonfiction insect books, and information discovered should be displayed on chart paper.

Teachers need to have lively, entertaining music ready to go before beginning this activity. Students can be placed in groups of four or five. Each group should have a hunter, and the other children in each group can choose an insect to pantomime. Teachers should have the students name the insects they've chosen and ask them how that insect defends itself, allowing students to check the research books or chart for accuracy.

When the teacher puts on the music, the hunter pretends to be coming for the insects, and the insects must act out the proper defense mechanism for their chosen insect while trying not to be tagged by the hunter. Tagged insects must sit down. Each time the music stops, the hunter and insects must freeze in place.

MOVEMENT ACTIVITIES 13–15: SCREEN-FREE BRAIN BREAKS

Materials

- None

Skills

- A variety of locomotor and nonlocomotor skills

Strategy

Any time students are feeling restless and struggling to pay attention, it's important for teachers to allow their kids to have a "brain break." Each of the following suggestions for movement breaks will only take a few minutes, and then everyone can get back to their regular schedule with the students ready to focus on the lesson at hand.

Activity 13: Mingle, Mingle, Group!

In this activity, students move around the classroom saying "mingle, mingle, mingle" in soft voices until the teacher says "groups of five," at which point the students must quickly assemble into groups with the correct number of people. Students who are left over must do three jumping jacks before the next round starts. Teachers can call out any number for the group size, and rules can be added—for example, as soon as a group is complete, all members must form a line.

Activity 14: Name Moves

Students stand behind their chairs for this activity. Every student has a chance to say his or her name with a special movement he or she has created. For example, a student might say "Alex!" while dramatically pretending to hit a baseball with an imaginary baseball bat. After the student does his or her move, the rest of the class says the student's name in unison and imitates the move. This movement activity continues until everyone has had a turn. It's a fun way to get the students moving and also a great opportunity for self-expression and community building.

Activity 15: Would You Rather

For this simple and engaging movement activity, all teachers need to do is ask a "would you rather" question and have students show their choice by moving from one end of the room to the other. Teachers can ask a few volunteers to share their reasons for choosing their side for each question asked. The possibilities for "would you rather" questions are endless; here are some suggestions:

- Go on a cruise to many islands or go on an RV trip around the United States?

- Be Jack from *Jack and the Beanstalk* or Goldilocks from *The Three Bears*?
- Eat ice cream with strawberries or chocolate chips?
- Adopt a stray cat or a stray dog?
- Be a sports star or a rock star?
- Eat dinner with the president or a famous actor?
- Sleep in a bed or a sleeping bag at a sleepover?
- Swim in a pool or the ocean?
- Be a great big giant or a little tiny person?
- Have a longer recess or a longer lunch?

As all teachers know, children who get regular physical activity experience improvements not just in their fitness levels but in brain function too. Physical activity doesn't have to be in a recess or PE setting to be effective. When teachers take the time to plan movement activities, the impact is tremendous! Students are not only better focused, healthier, and ready to learn but also having so much fun!

> *Watching a child makes it obvious that the development of his mind comes through his movements.*
> —Maria Montessori

Chapter Ten

Lose the Clip Chart, Color Changer, and Sticker Chart

Fifteen Ways to Build Community with a Growth Mind-set Approach to Classroom Discipline

> *Relationships are the foundation with difficult kids. Every. Single. Time. Looking elsewhere (tickets, charts, etc . . .) wastes time and often makes things worse. Trust the process. Building valuable anything always takes longer than planned.*
>
> —Brian Mendler

Effective teachers know that classroom discipline should be handled with respect, kindness, consistency, and encouragement. They help students aspire to be their best selves and develop positive self-esteem. Their methods are focused on improving students' sense of responsibility and helping students develop a growth mind-set.

A growth mind-set is a belief that you can change and grow. It is an understanding that there are no bad kids or good kids. Students should be taught that there are people and strategies accessible to them that can help them learn. Many behavior plans, such as clip charts, color change charts, and sticker or reward systems, rely on the idea that kids know the behaviors and need to be prodded into using them.

When teachers give students the skills and strategies they need to achieve higher levels in reading and math, they are teaching them about that word *yet*. They highlight and compliment students' strengths and build on them while providing tools and techniques to help them progress. Teachers don't get upset with students or take each mistake as a personal attack. They don't bribe students to solve a math problem correctly because they know the student would solve it if he or she could. Effective teachers help students realize that although they haven't mastered a skill *yet*, they have the power to persevere and will achieve their goals in time.

A growth mind-set applied to behavior is about setting goals for how students will act, giving them strategies to use in new and challenging situations, and helping students reflect on their actions and outcomes. Instead of shaming or bribing students by using a behavior management system that involves publicly clipping down, changing colors, or adding stickers to a chart, there are many better ways teachers can promote positive behavior and a classroom culture of mutual respect and understanding.

BETTER WAY TO PROMOTE POSITIVE BEHAVIOR 1: PREVENTION

Effective teachers spend more time establishing strategies for preventing problems than they spend on handling behavior issues. Good classroom management involves established routines, consistent implementation of carefully negotiated rules, careful lesson planning, and smooth transitions between lessons and activities. Planning effective instructional strategies, such as giving students choices, catering to students' needs and interests, addressing different learning styles, and keeping kids actively engaged, will prevent many undesirable classroom behaviors.

BETTER WAY TO PROMOTE POSITIVE BEHAVIOR 2: TAKE YOUR EGO OUT OF THE CLASSROOM

It's important for teachers to have self-confidence and not feel defensive or authoritarian when students have a complaint or display inappropriate behaviors. Effective teachers realize that the student is having a hard time, not purposely giving anyone else a hard time or acting out because he or she dislikes a teacher.

BETTER WAY TO PROMOTE POSITIVE BEHAVIOR 3: POSITIVITY

Students need and respond well to teachers who like and respect them. Getting to know students, establishing a good rapport, showing a sincere interest in their lives, and communicating that students are valued are all tremendously important in promoting positive behavior in every classroom.

BETTER WAY TO PROMOTE POSITIVE BEHAVIOR 4: EXPECTATIONS

Effective teachers help students see themselves as capable, responsible people, and in response students act that way. When setting expectations, it's important for teachers to address individual differences. However, there are specific ways teachers can take differences into consideration, communicate high expectations, and encourage more productive and positive behavior.

Effective teachers do the following:

- Give sincere and specific praise.
- Make eye contact and listen to what they say when students speak, .
- Rephrase rules and directions and constantly remind students of the correct behavior.
- Respond positively to all behavior by either affirming great choices or correcting and redirecting the students to change their behavior.
- Model the respect and kindness they expect students to return.
- Encourage students to set their own behavior goals.
- Stay sensitive to the emotional needs of students.
- Give students enough time to respond to a redirection.
- Ask themselves if they are unfairly judging a child because of a report or opinion from a previous year.

BETTER WAY TO PROMOTE POSITIVE BEHAVIOR 5: BE PRESENT

Without exception, effective teachers are aware of what is happening in the classroom at all times. They regularly and actively monitor all areas of the classroom and position themselves where they can see all students. They let their students know they are present and aware at all times.

BETTER WAY TO PROMOTE POSITIVE BEHAVIOR 6: SAY NO TO CLIQUES

Offering cooperative activities such as the ones shared throughout this book will encourage group identity and a sense of community and also discourage cliques and other antisocial behavior.

BETTER WAY TO PROMOTE POSITIVE BEHAVIOR 7: RESPECT CULTURAL DIFFERENCES

Effective teachers take the time to be aware of cultural differences. Certain behaviors may be respectful in some cultures, such as not looking at a teacher when he or she speaks, but could appear defiant in others.

BETTER WAY TO PROMOTE POSITIVE BEHAVIOR 8: BE SPECIFIC

It's important to be consistent and also very specific when helping students understand why a misbehavior is not acceptable. Students need to be taught to reflect on the behavior and think about how they could avoid allowing the same thing to happen again. Very young students may need explanations modeled.

BETTER WAY TO PROMOTE POSITIVE BEHAVIOR 9: BE DISCRETE

Teachers who value a culture of kindness and a community built on trust and respect, who believe that educating the heart is a priority, will speak to students about their behavior in private. Embarrassing a child is never an option for a truly effective teacher.

BETTER WAY TO PROMOTE POSITIVE BEHAVIOR 10: LISTEN

Active listening must be part of any classroom's plan for positive behavior success. Students should be encouraged to talk about their feelings and concerns. Often they may need to be asked to restate or clarify their statements. It's important for teachers to take the time to really understand what students are thinking and work on honest, open communication every day. It's never appropriate to be judgmental when children are sharing their thoughts. Effective teachers model honest and open communication.

BETTER WAY TO PROMOTE POSITIVE BEHAVIOR 11: ADDRESS ACADEMIC SURVIVAL

Because effective teachers know that many unpleasant classroom behaviors stem from academic confusion or not being challenged appropriately, they constantly differentiate instruction and adapt activities so students are neither bored nor struggling. Teachers also work hard to ensure students have schoolwork survival skills such as paying attention, following directions, asking for help when needed, volunteering to answer, and extending their learning.

BETTER WAY TO PROMOTE POSITIVE BEHAVIOR 12: CALM CORNER

It's essential for every classroom to have a corner or space designated as the "calm corner." A calm corner is a valuable tool to have in a classroom for students to use and improve their self-regulation skills. All students should have an area and opportunity to calm themselves down when upset and cheer themselves up when they are down. It's crucial for students to be able to release anger and engage their mind without feeling threatened or as if they are "in trouble." A calm corner is not a punishment and should not be used as a time out.

Calm corners are most effective when catered to the individual needs of the students in the classroom. Teachers will often create individual shoebox-

es for each student. Each shoebox will contain items chosen specifically for what the student needs to calm down or cheer up. Items can include stuffed animals, sensory items such as colorful rice scented with lavender, calming glitter jars, engaging books, soothing music, or even just crayons and paper.

When students feel a need to visit the calm corner, they can take their own individual box, which has been filled with supplies just for them, and have the time and space they need to get back on track and ready to focus and learn.

BETTER WAY TO PROMOTE POSITIVE BEHAVIOR 13: WORD CHOICE

Teachers have the power to set the most positive tone possible by being mindful of their word choice. The language of discipline should be as carefully planned as the language and vocabulary used in academic lessons. In a positive learning atmosphere, positive language should be substituted, whenever possible, for negative language while keeping the focus on the desired behavior. For example, "Look this way and listen, thank you!" is better than saying "Don't talk while I'm teaching." Telling students to "Share the center supplies fairly" is better than saying "Don't argue and fight over the pencils."

BETTER WAY TO PROMOTE POSITIVE BEHAVIOR 14: NONVERBAL LANGUAGE AWARENESS

It's not only the words teachers say that matter, it's also the tone of voice, eye contact, body language, and proximity to students that affect how words are perceived and how effective they can be in helping students meet positive behavior expectations.

Effective teachers are careful to do the following:

- Balance correction with encouragement, and focus on reestablishing working relationships.
- Focus on the behavior; never attack the person.
- Attain a state of calm before trying to calm a student.
- Address issues that really count rather than waste time and energy on minor issues that don't really matter.
- Be brief when addressing behavior, even when using commands.

BETTER WAY TO PROMOTE POSITIVE BEHAVIOR 15: LOVE YOUR STUDENTS

There is absolutely no quick fix. Whatever words teachers use or techniques they try, positive discipline educates the heart of a child, providing him or her with a daily dose of caring. These long-term efforts will send the message, "You are a good person; you are worthy of respect and capable of self-discipline." Effective teachers love their students unconditionally, show them they care day after day, and never give up.

> *You can't hang behavior charts/color clips etc . . . on the wall and ask/tell kids to mind their own business.*
>
> —Brian Mendler

Chapter Eleven

Homework — Make It Meaningful

Fifteen Ways to Keep Kids Engaged and Encourage Authentic Learning at Home

> *To develop a complete mind, study the science of art; study the art of science. Learn how to see. Realize that everything connects to everything else.*
> —Leonardo da Vinci

Motivation is the key to authentic learning. Great teachers cater to the individual interests, natural curiosity, and personal desires of students with effective strategies to inspire students' increased growth, learning, and overall well-being. Homework strategies that integrate instruction, allow students to make choices about what they learn, encourage creativity, value thinking skills, and ask excellent questions for students to explore in imaginative ways will motivate students to be engaged, successful learners at home.

Homework should never be busywork, punishment, or a way for students to teach themselves. It should always have clear expectations, be an opportunity for students to take ownership of their learning, allow for multiple pathways to success, and be connected to real-life situations.

These homework ideas can be adapted to accommodate any grade level and are a wonderful way to meaningfully integrate subjects. They are not meant to be completed in one night or even a weekend. Students should be allowed time to choose a topic of interest, plan, and create. Three to four weeks is recommended. The completed projects and assignments are meant to be shared with the whole class, allowing for awesome community-building discourse opportunities.

HOMEWORK PROJECT 1: GAME CREATION

Recommended Grade Range

Grades 1–6

Students should choose a topic and create a new game based on important facts or concepts about the topic. It could be a board game, athletic game, card game, or any other type of game they can think of. For example, younger students might create an alphabet card game, and older students might make a board game in which students answer questions about the United States.

HOMEWORK PROJECT 2: MUSIC MAKER

Recommended Grade Range

PreK–Grade 6

Students should choose a topic or concept and create lyrics about it that they can connect to the tune of a popular song. The lyrics should be carefully thought out to show understanding of the topic or concept and should teach the class new information.

HOMEWORK PROJECT 3: WHO AM I?

Recommended Grade Range

Grades 1–6

Students should choose a famous person and write a report they will present to the class, pretending to be that person. They can create a hat or prop to make their presentation more engaging. The goal should be for the other students to guess who they are without knowing the famous person's name.

HOMEWORK PROJECT 4: THE MOST MEMORABLE DAY

Recommended Grade Range

Grades 1–6

Students should think of a day in their life that was memorable and write a diary entry re-creating the day. They should include the date and a chronological listing of times that different events occurred during the day and provide as many details as possible. Students should include either photographs or drawn pictures and any other type of memorabilia or souvenir that would show the class why the day was so memorable.

HOMEWORK PROJECT 5: COMMUNITY HELPER SPOTLIGHT

Recommended Grade Range

PreK–Grade 6

Students should think about the different helpers in their community and choose one to interview. They should create their own questions and be able to explain to the class why they selected the person they did and how he or she benefits the community. They should include photographs or drawn pictures and any other type of artifact that would help to show something unique about the community helper.

HOMEWORK PROJECT 6: RECIPE INNOVATION

Recommended Grade Range

Grades 1–6

Students should take a basic favorite recipe and change one part of it to make it unique. For example, they could add peanut butter to a pancake recipe or slices of pineapple to homemade pizza. They should write a report explaining how the recipe is usually prepared and their reasons for deciding on their innovation. They should explain the tools they used, how they measured ingredients, and discuss whether the end result was as expected. They should have photographs or drawn pictures and tell whether they feel the recipe was worth making again. It would be awesome if the students could provide a copy of their recipe innovation for each of their classmates.

HOMEWORK PROJECT 7: KINDNESS CHALLENGE

Recommended Grade Range

PreK–Grade 6

Students should be given a blank monthly calendar and attempt to perform a random act of kindness each day. They should record a kind act on each day of the calendar and also write (or draw for younger students) details, such as who they were kind to, how they felt, and how they think the other person felt. Students should share a summary of their month, discussing their favorite ideas for being kind and their favorite responses from people they were kind to.

HOMEWORK PROJECT 8: STICKING TO A BUDGET

Recommended Grade Range

Grades 2–6

Students should be given a budget and a choice list of purposes for shopping at a local store. They can decide if they want to shop for food for a celebration, warm clothes for a children's shelter, or cleaning supplies for the classroom. The options are endless, and this project can very easily be differentiated by changing the budget total. Students should prepare a shopping list with items and price estimates and then go to the store and find out how much the items they chose actually cost and how much the total would be. They could be challenged to find out what prices and totals would be if certain items were on sale. For example, they could be asked to pretend there was a buy one, get one half off sale, or that everything in the store was 25% off.

HOMEWORK PROJECT 9: A HISTORICAL MOMENT FROZEN IN TIME

Recommended Grade Range

Grades 1–6

Students should think of a meaningful moment in history and re-create it inside a shoebox or shadow box to show it "frozen" in time. They can be asked to also provide a written report in the form of a newspaper article, pretending it is the date the moment occurred.

HOMEWORK PROJECT 10: CEREAL BOX BOOK COVER

Recommended Grade Range

PreK–Grade 6

Students can choose any book they love and design a book cover out of a cereal (or some other type of food) box. They should be expected to show the title, author, and a picture that captures the essence of the book on the front as well as a synopsis and review on the back.

HOMEWORK PROJECT 11: ANIMAL WATCHING

Recommended Grade Range

PreK–Grade 6

Students should be asked to observe an animal for at least an hour. It could be a neighborhood cat, a family dog, a squirrel, or even an insect or a worm. They need to describe it in full detail, discussing appearance, sounds, and all activity. They can write their observations in the form of a poem, a short story, or as a scientific journal observation entry.

HOMEWORK PROJECT 12: THE PERFECT VACATION

Recommended Grade Range

Grades 1–6

Students should think of a location for the perfect one-week vacation and plan an itinerary. They need to find out how far away the place is, the best

way to travel there, and what the weather will be. They can find out the types of food and restaurants that are available and the best tourist attractions. Students could also show what they would pack by drawing and labeling items inside a file folder "suitcase."

HOMEWORK PROJECT 13: SCAVENGER HUNT

Recommended Grade Range

PreK–Grade 6

Students should be given a list of items to find on an at-home scavenger hunt. Items on the list should not be specific; they should be descriptive. Asking students to find something quiet, something hilarious, something beautiful, or something frightening will allow for many opportunities for students to be creative and make their own choices. They could take photos of the items and create short captions for each one, write a report discussing each of the items they found, or use their imagination and write a fictional story including each of the items on the list.

HOMEWORK PROJECT 14: BE THE TEACHER

Recommended Grade Range

Grades 1–6

Students need to choose a topic or concept to teach the class. It should be something they consider themselves to be an "expert" on. Some students might choose to teach about a hobby, such as collecting baseball cards, playing a musical instrument, or constructing mini figure settings with building bricks. Other students might choose to expand on a theme or topic being studied in school, such as the solar system or the United States. They should decide on at least five facts to teach the class about their subject and create a quiz to give the class when their presentation is complete.

HOMEWORK PROJECT 15: MY LIFE IN COMICS

Recommended Grade Range

PreK–Grade 6

Students should create a comic strip or entire comic book based on their life. They could create a panel for each year of their life, include several strips for each year, or make it as simple as three panels showing birth, kid, adult (if futuristic). Teachers should, as always, make expectations clear and specific yet leave lots of room for creativity, choice, and self-expression.

SUMMARY

These meaningful homework projects are not meant to be assigned in addition to busywork, as work meant for students to teach themselves, as punishment, or as work students did not finish at school. These projects are intended to replace these practices and give the students opportunities to take ownership of their learning, apply learned skills, be creative, improve communication and critical-thinking skills, and contribute to the classroom community.

It is a miracle that curiosity survives formal education.
—Albert Einstein

Chapter Twelve

The Communities Beyond Your Classroom Community

Fifteen Ways to Build Relationships that Support Meaningful Learning

> *Community is much more than belonging to something; it's about doing something together that makes belonging matter.*
> —Brian Solis

Students need to have hope. When children believe in themselves and their power to bring good into the world, they will be more apt to seek out knowledge and choose activities that help them learn and grow. Teachers can help students to see themselves as valued members of a larger community by providing an environment of comfort and growth, encouraging individuality, and helping them connect with individuals and groups beyond the classroom doors.

The relationships teachers build should be purposeful with the learning and well-being of the students as the priority. Children need to express their curiosity, learn to interact with others in positive and productive ways, have confidence to think independently, and have the courage to do the right thing in different situations. The ideas in this chapter will positively affect students because they encourage meaningful connections and experiences and allow for independent thinking and originality.

CONNECTION BEYOND THE CLASSROOM IDEA 1: PROFESSIONAL LEARNING COMMUNITY WITH A PURPOSE

When teachers work together with a defined purpose, open and honest communication, and a collegial mind-set, either as a grade-level team or in a vertical way, with every grade level and special subject represented, students will ultimately benefit in powerful ways. A professional learning community (PLC) should be more than a group of teachers getting together to discuss an article or book they've read; it should be an ongoing process of examining instructional practices and student benchmarks, consistent reflection, and monitoring of outcomes.

One way to make this work and ensure that students' needs are the priority is to take a critical look at the learning expectations for a group of students. The PLC can then select evidence-based instructional strategies that they feel will help students meet the standard and also allow for differentiation, critical-thinking skills, communication, and creativity. The team should agree on a lesson plan and the type of student work that will be collected. Once the lesson is implemented and work is complete, the PLC should then discuss successes and challenges and decide on ways to improve instruction to increase student learning. The conversation should focus on essential questions about learning, real-life data, and observations and be based on current, applicable research.

CONNECTION BEYOND THE CLASSROOM IDEA 2: SCHOOLWIDE "WALL OF WONDER" COLLABORATIVE ART PROJECT

Materials

- *Wonder* by R. J. Palacio (Knopf Books for Young Readers, 2012)
- *We're All Wonders* by R. J. Palacio (Knopf Books for Young Readers, 2017)
- 1 small stretched canvas for every student in the school
- Acrylic paint and paintbrushes
- Nails or adhesive-type hooks for hanging the completed canvases

Students from every classroom in the school will be able to express themselves artistically and feel an enormous sense of pride as they contribute to the entire community by creating a canvas for a "wall of wonder." Using small stretched canvases, students can paint their own designs based on the theme "wonder." Either *Wonder* or *We're All Wonders* by R. J. Palacio, depending on age level, should be read and discussed first. The quote "Look with kindness and you will always find wonder" can be highlighted as the concept of individuality, and the idea that we are all "wonders" is presented. The students can then paint something that represents their uniqueness on their canvas, and all artwork should be displayed in an orderly fashion.

CONNECTION BEYOND THE CLASSROOM IDEA 3: NATIVE AMERICAN HERITAGE NIGHT

November is Native American Heritage Month, but any time of the year would be great for students to focus on the heritage and culture of Native Americans and culminate their work by putting together a special night for parents. Each grade level or class could research and study different regions or tribes and create reports, replicas, artwork, recipes, clothing representations, dramatizations of legends, and games based on their learning. Students will love sharing their projects and learning from the other classrooms and grade levels. Families and community members can be invited, and it would also be wonderful to have authentic Native American tribal members attend as guests or even as performers and speakers if possible.

CONNECTION BEYOND THE CLASSROOM IDEA 4: FAMILY "SLEEPOVER" STORY NIGHT

The whole school can work together to plan an evening full of literature-based "sleepover" activities that families will love being a part of. Every grade level should work together to choose a book with a bedtime theme and activities for students and families to engage in throughout the event. Although it's called a "sleepover," the event is really only meant to be an hour or so in the evening, not for families to actually sleep at the school. It would be really fun if children and even teachers and staff dressed in pajamas. Some schools hold their story night when they have a book fair or PTO meeting planned to encourage participation and improve family engagement at other meetings.

Book and Activity Suggestions

- *Llama, Llama, Red Pajama* by Anna Dewdney (Viking, 2005): Students can be given paper-doll templates, craft sticks, and a variety of arts-and-crafts scraps and supplies to create puppets of themselves wearing pajamas.
- *Ira Sleeps Over* by Bernard Waber (Sandpiper, 1975): Students can be given construction paper or card stock that they can fold, cut, and decorate to make it look like an overnight bag. They can then draw and label items

inside that they think they would like to take with them on an actual sleepover. Another alterative would be for students to look in magazines for items to cut out and then glue inside their pretend overnight bag.
- *Fancy Nancy Saturday Night Sleepover* by Jane O'Connor (HarperCollins, 2016): This is a great story to initiate a discussion of feelings and how we can help each other not be nervous when doing new things. Students can create "fancy" speech bubbles out of paper or card stock with kind, reassuring phrases they would use to help someone feel less nervous about something new they need to do.
- *Mallory's Super Sleepover* by Laura Friedman (Darby Creek, 2012): Students can decorate premade cupcakes with frosting and sprinkles for a special "sleepover" treat!

CONNECTION BEYOND THE CLASSROOM IDEA 5: MULTICULTURAL DAY

Teachers and staff can work together to plan a day to celebrate the variety of cultures within their school. On that day, students, families, and community members could have the opportunity to share their own cultural identity and also learn about the differences and similarities of other classmates. Participants could choose to bring in food, authentic clothes, or artifacts or create a poster with pictures and information to present. They should all be encouraged to speak about their culture and ask thoughtful, respectful questions to other classmates who choose to share.

An alternate way to have a multicultural day is to have different classrooms or grade levels research and prepare presentations with food, pictures, and information about different cultures. Often teachers will plan to do this during different months to make it easy for the rest of the classrooms to learn from each other. For example, the third graders might study Guatemalan culture during the month of January and invite their families and the rest of the school to attend their presentation. They might decide to prepare and serve *torrijas* (Guatemalan French toast) and share traditional stories and customs that they researched. Fifth graders might study Mexican culture in March, prepare Mexican chocolate pudding, and even create an authentic piñata for their celebration.

CONNECTION BEYOND THE CLASSROOM IDEA 6: WELLNESS FAIR

Organizing a wellness or health fair is a worthwhile endeavor that will give families the opportunity to visit the school, meet their children's teachers, and help them see the school as a community resource. It's a wonderful way

to share information about physical activity, healthy eating, and local health services.

Many schools reach out to community partners who are often quite honored to be included in school health and wellness events. Local chefs and nutritionists can be asked to demonstrate easy, nutritious, and affordable recipes. Local dairy councils may be able to provide nutrition education resources, and local chapters of the American Heart Association, American Lung Association, American Diabetes Association, American Cancer Society, and Alzheimer's Association may provide wellness information and free services, such as blood pressure and vision screenings.

Schools often plan their health and wellness fair in the late afternoon to early evening hours so parents that pick up their children right when the dismissal bell rings can attend first, and then others who may work late will be available to participate toward the end. Providing healthy snacks is definitely recommended, and some schools also offer door prizes donated by local businesses to encourage greater attendance and involvement in the event.

CONNECTION BEYOND THE CLASSROOM IDEA 7: BEST BOOK BALLOON LAUNCH

A best book balloon launch is an amazing way to involve the entire school, connect with people around the country, and increase excitement about books. Every child will need a balloon and a small piece of paper. Each child should write down the best book he or she has ever read, his or her classroom number and school address, and a request that whoever finds the balloon send back a letter or postcard stating where the balloon was found.

The notes should be laminated and cut with rounded edges to avoid puncturing the balloon. A hole needs to be punched into each card, and then they can be tied to strings of helium-filled balloons. This should all be done inside to be sure students do not lose their balloons during the card-tying process.

When all the students have their balloons ready for launch, the entire school should go out to the schoolyard, and with lots of drama and fanfare, there should be a group countdown. Ten . . . nine . . . eight . . . seven . . . six . . . five . . . four . . . three . . . two . . . one . . . book balloons away! It's exciting for the students to see the balloons soar until they are out of sight. It's even more exciting when postcards start coming in from different towns, cities, and even states! Many schools have a large map of the United States in the school cafeteria or library so classrooms can keep track of the postcards they receive. Many times classrooms write back to the balloon recipients and establish pen pal relationships.

CONNECTION BEYOND THE CLASSROOM IDEA 8: POETRY CAFÉ

April is National Poetry Month and would be a great time to have students write poems and read them to the entire community in an authentic poetry café setting. The poetry café can be set up in any common area of the school. Small tables with café-style tablecloths and stools, a stage made out of plastic risers or any type of platform that will put students slightly higher than the audience, a microphone, and maybe a lamp is all that is needed to set the stage.

Families can be asked to provide light refreshments, and students can create advertisements and programs to invite and welcome community members. Students can all present their poems in one event or be assigned different days for a designated "poetry week." Some schools have had a lot of success and fun when asking parents, siblings, and community members to come up to an "open mic" in between the students' poetry readings to share their own favorite poems from a variety of books made available for this purpose.

CONNECTION BEYOND THE CLASSROOM IDEA 9: MUSEUM OUTREACH PROGRAMS

Many schools have had to reduce or even eliminate museum trips, either because of small budgets that make it difficult to pay for a bus and museum admission or because of limited time in the schedule because of mandates from the district or state. Fortunately, many museums offer traveling programs, teaching lessons right in classrooms and using their collections as tools. Students can learn about astronomy, paleontology, and just about any topic from an expert with hands-on artifacts. They will experience so much more excitement, wonder, and authentic learning than they ever could with a Google search.

CONNECTION BEYOND THE CLASSROOM IDEA 10: REAL-LIFE LEARNING: JOURNALISTS AND LAWYERS

Teachers can invite professionals from the community to visit their classroom to show students the relevance of what they are learning and how their knowledge can be applied to real-world jobs and tasks. A lawyer can explain the importance of constructing a viable argument, and a journalist can help students understand how important it is to check facts and provide quality, accurate information to readers.

CONNECTION BEYOND THE CLASSROOM IDEA 11: INTERVIEWING INSPIRING NEIGHBORS

Students can interview and write a story about a person in their family or community who is at least a generation older than they are. They should share the person's stories, emphasizing their youth, cultural heritage, and philanthropic efforts. Students should all reflect on the positive impact each person interviewed has made in the community and ways they are inspired to also make a difference.

Alternatively, teachers can choose to invite these family members and neighbors to speak to the class about their culture, memories of challenges and successes, and how they have contributed to society. Students may ask the speakers carefully thought-out questions and later write them letters to thank them for their visit and inspiration.

Figure 12.2.

CONNECTION BEYOND THE CLASSROOM IDEA 12: THE POWER OF THE PUBLIC LIBRARY

The impact of collaborating with the public library must not be overlooked. Even students who are regular visitors to the library will gain new excitement about all it has to offer when they visit with their school. They can be introduced to new areas and programs they may not have been aware of and also gain a new comfort level with the environment and people. Many libraries offer special free programs for school groups and also welcome the opportunity to visit classrooms.

Some branches have fabulous art and history programs that help students explore their neighborhoods with topics such as urban architecture, rights and voting, and transportation. There are also librarians who will come to schools with equipment and supplies to help students perform science experiments about topics they are currently studying.

Another popular library program involves students exploring different cities with books and activities and then gives the children many opportunities to build bridges, design cars, and create monuments based on their experiences. Teachers and librarians who take the time to collaborate are able to create meaningful, memorable moments for children that truly inspire authentic learning.

CONNECTION BEYOND THE CLASSROOM IDEA 13: PARTNER WITH CIVIC GROUPS

Partnerships that are established between students, educators, and civic agencies can lead to beautiful, sustainable relationships, offering strong support and inspiring authentic learning. The Boy Scouts, local business clubs such as the Rotary and the Kiwanis, Boys and Girls Clubs, the YMCA, and recreational sports leagues in the community are all organizations that have worked with schools successfully.

These connections work best when students and educators serve as equal partners with the civic group and work toward an established goal. One idea is to promote lifelong healthy eating habits and connect students to the natural world by working together with a civic group to start a garden. The nationwide growth of farm-to-school programs has inspired many forms of gardens in schools, from simple container gardens to raised beds to acres of plowed land.

The process of starting a garden in a school community requires careful planning, but it is well worth the effort. Taking the time to form a committee, establish goals, design, fund, connect to the classroom, plant, and enjoy the harvest is a worthwhile way to encourage practical, real-life, hands-on, inquiry-based learning and experimentation.

CONNECTION BEYOND THE CLASSROOM IDEA 14: ADOPT A SPOT TO SPREAD KINDNESS

Students and teachers can make a huge difference in the everyday lives of so many when they "adopt a spot." It can be as simple as a classroom creating artwork connected to their favorite quotes about kindness for a spot where parents and educational specialists meet to collaborate on individualized education programs. One teacher and second grade class from an inner-city public school did this to spread some joy in a main district building that needed a little bit of love and cheerfulness. The students who created the work and the adults who got to see it every day felt such a connection that they became pen pals!

In can be as complex as students, teachers, support staff, families, and volunteers from the community making a commitment to take care of a local area within a park, hiking trail, a courtyard at a library, a municipal building, or a planting area near a hospital. They can decide on several dates throughout the year to meet and perform a variety of cleaning and beautification tasks. Tasks might include picking up litter, weeding, painting, removing graffiti, and reporting unsafe conditions and more complicated maintenance needs.

CONNECTION BEYOND THE CLASSROOM IDEA 15: GET INVOLVED, HELP OTHERS, AND MAKE A DIFFERENCE

Students and teachers can connect with others by looking for opportunities to help people in need. There are many nonprofit organizations that make it easy for schools to help, such as the Muscular Dystrophy Association with their annual Hop-a-Thon initiative and the Leukemia and Lymphoma Society, who give hope to kids fighting cancer with their Pennies for Patients program.

Students can bring smiles to senior citizens by visiting an assisted living or nursing home facility. They might sing songs, create artwork, or work on puzzles with the residents.

SUMMARY

When teachers help students connect with individuals and groups beyond the classroom doors, they give them opportunities to see themselves as valued members of society, express their individuality, and grow in a supportive environment.

> *How wonderful it is that nobody need wait a single moment before starting to improve the world.*
> —Anne Frank

Appendix

Book List

CHAPTER 1

In My Heart: A Book of Feelings by Jo Witek
The Color Monster: A Story about Emotions by Anna Zlenas
My Many Colored Days by Dr. Seuss
Charlotte's Web by E. B. White

CHAPTER 3

Goodnight Moon by Margaret Wise Brown
Brown Bear, Brown Bear, What Do You See? by Eric Carle
The Very Hungry Caterpillar by Eric Carle
The Lemonade War by Jacqueline Davie
Alexander, Who Used to Be Rich Last Sunday by Judith Viorst
Where the Sidewalk Ends by Shel Silverstein
Johnny Appleseed by Steven Kellogg
Rosie's Walk by Pat Hutchins
The Doorbell Rang by Pat Hutchins
The Wolf's Chicken Stew by Keiko Kasza
Eating the Alphabet by Lois Ehlert
The Teddy Bears' Picnic by Jimmy Kennedy
Henry and Mudge in Puddle Trouble by Cynthia Rylant
Purple, Green, and Yellow by Robert Munsch
Something Special for Me by Vera B. Williams
The Gingerbread Man Loose at the Zoo by Laura Murray

The Principal's New Clothes by Stephanie Calmenson
Take Me Out to the Ballgame by Jack Norworth
The Three Little Pigs by Paul Galdone
The Very Busy Spider by Eric Carle
The Very Lonely Firefly by Eric Carle
Who Sank the Boat? by Pamela Allen

CHAPTER 4

Where the Sidewalk Ends by Shel Silverstein
A Light in the Attic by Shel Silverstein
No More Homework! No More Tests!: Kids' Favorite Funny School Poems by Bruce Lansky
Honey, I Love and Other Poems (Reading Rainbow Series) by Eloise Greenfield
Tomie dePaola's Mother Goose by Tomie dePaola
The 20th Century Children's Poetry Treasury by Jack Prelutsky
National Geographic Little Kids First Big Book of Who (National Geographic Little Kids First Big Books) by Jill Esbaum
Who Was Walt Disney? (Who Was?) by Whitney Stewart
Who Was Albert Einstein? (Who Was?) by Jess Brallier
Rising Above: How 11 Athletes Overcame Challenges in Their Youth to Become Stars by Gregory Zuckerman
The Big Book of Presidents: From George Washington to Barack Obama by Nancy J. Hajeski
Women in Science: 50 Fearless Pioneers Who Changed the World by Rachel Ignotofsky
Me on the Map (Rise and Shine) by National Geographic Learning
National Geographic Kids World Atlas, Fifth Edition by National Geographic Kids
Maps of the World: An Illustrated Children's Atlas of Adventure, Culture, and Discovery by Enrico Lavagno
Where on Earth?: The Ultimate Atlas of What's Where in the World by DK
The Everything Kids' Geography Book: From the Grand Canyon to the Great Barrier Reef—Explore the World! by Jane P. Gardner
Maps and Globes by Jack Knowlton
The Celebrity Black Book 2015, by contactanycelebrity.com
The Golden Book of Fairy Tales (Golden Classics) by Adrienne Segur
The Post Office Book: Mail and How It Moves by Gail Gibbons
Dear Mr. Blueberry by Simon James
A Letter to Amy by Ezra Jack Keats

Dear Juno by Soyung Pak
Don't Forget to Write by Martina Selway
Dear Mr. Henshaw by Beverly Cleary
The Cloud Book by Tomie dePaola
National Geographic Backyard Guide to the Birds of North America by Jonathan Alderfer
The Reasons for Seasons by Gail Gibbons
Watching the Seasons (Welcome Books: Watching Nature) by Edana Eckart
The Kids' Book of Weather Forecasting (Kids Can!) by Mark Breen
Oh Say Can You Say What's the Weather Today? All about Weather (Cat in the Hat's Learning Library) by Tish Rabe
A Backyard Birding Adventure: What's in Your Yard? by Kermit Cummings
Backyard Bugs: An Identification Guide to Common Insects, Spiders, and More by Jaret C. Daniels
Stay Away from the Junkyard! by Tricia Tusa
The Caboose Who Got Loose by Bill Peet
The Mouse and the Motorcycle by Beverly Cleary
Crafting with Recyclables (How-to Library) by Dana Meachen Rau
Recyclables (Make It With . . .) by Anna Llimaos Plomer
DK Eyewitness Books: Train: Discover the Story of Railroads from the Age of Steam to the High-Speed Trains of Today by John Coiley
Steam, Smoke, and Steel: Back in Time with Trains by Patrick O'Brien
Motorcycles for Kids: A Children's Picture Book about Motorcycles: A Great Simple Picture Book for Kids to Learn about Different Types of Motorcycles by Melissa Ackerman
Motorcycles! (Step into Reading) by Susan E. Goodman
The Way I Feel by Janan Cain
What Should Danny Do? (The Power to Choose) by Adir Levy
Even Superheroes Have Bad Days by Shelly Becker
Be Kind by Pat Zietlow Miller
Visiting Feelings by Lauren Rubenstein
Alexander and the Terrible, Horrible, No Good, Very Bad Day by Judith Viorst
Magic Tree House Series by Mary Pope Osborne
Encyclopedia Brown Series by Donald J. Sobol
Rebekah—Girl Detective Books 1–8: Fun Short Story Mysteries for Children Ages 9–12 by P. J. Ryan
Ada Lace, On the Case by Emily Calandrelli
The Boxcar Children Series by Gertrude Chandler Warner
Nancy Drew Mystery Series by Carolyn Keene

Jokes for Kids: The Best Jokes, Riddles, Tongue Twisters, Knock-Knock Jokes, and One-liners for Kids by Rob Stevens
Laugh-Out-Loud Jokes for Kids by Rob Elliott
Ridiculous Riddles by National Geographic Kids
Knock Knock! The Biggest, Best Joke Book Ever (Highlights Laugh Attack! Joke Books) by Highlights
Seriously Silly Jokes for Kids: Joke Book for Boys and Girls Ages 7–12 (Volume 1) by Wally Brown
Best Joke Book for Kids: Best Funny Jokes and Knock-Knock Jokes (200+ Jokes) by Peter MacDonald
100 Things to Be When You Grow Up by Lisa M. Gerry
When I Grow Up by Tim Minchin
The Future Architect's Handbook by Barbara Beck
Metamorphosis of Medicine (Time for Kids Nonfiction Readers) by Sharon Coan
I Want to Be a Doctor by Laura Driscoll
All in a Day's Work: Police Officer (Time for Kids Nonfiction Readers by Diana Herweck
Busy People: Police Officer by Lucy M. George
Action! Making Movies (Time for Kids Nonfiction Readers) by Sarah Garza
Enhancing Engineering (Time for Kids Nonfiction Readers) by Wendy Conklin
STEM Careers: Reinventing Robotics (Time Nonfiction Readers) by Saskia Lacey
Today I'm a Veterinarian by Marisa Polansky
Workers Who Take Care of Me (Time for Kids Nonfiction Readers) by Sharon Coan
National Geographic Readers: Helpers in Your Neighborhood (Pre-reader) by Shira Evans
Liberty or Death: The American Revolution: 1763–1783 by Betsy Maestro
Reader's Theater: Folk and Fairy Tales English Set (Classroom Library Collections) by Teacher Created Materials
On Stage Theater Games and Activities for Kids by Lisa Bany-Winters
Acting Scenes and Monologues for Kids! Original Scenes and Monologues Combined into One Very Special Book! by Bo Kane
Cinderella Outgrows the Glass Slipper and Other Zany Fractured Fairy Tale Plays by Joan M. Wolf
Kids Are So Dramatic Monologues: Volume 1 by Tracey Ann Ball
American Tall Tales by Mary Pope Osborne
Daily Life in a Covered Wagon by Paul Erickson

A Kid's Life during the Westward Expansion (How Kids Lived) by Sarah Machajewski
If You Traveled West in a Covered Wagon by Ellen Levine
Abraham Lincoln: From the Log Cabin to the White House: Campfire Heroes Line (Campfire Graphic Novels, 2013) by Lewis Helfand
Journey of a Pioneer by Patricia J. Murphy
The Quilt Story by Tony Johnston
Pioneer Cat (A Stepping Stone Book) by William H. Hooks
The Little House Cookbook: Frontier Foods from Laura Ingalls Wilder's Classic Stories by Barbara M. Walker
If You Were a Kid on the Oregon Trail by Josh Gregory
Pioneer Days: Discover the Past with Fun Projects, Games, Activities, and Recipes (American Kids in History) by David C. King
Charlie the Ranch Dog: Charlie's Snow Day by Ree Drummond
Your Life as a Pioneer on the Oregon Trail (The Way It Was) by Jessica Gunderson
Heading West: Life with the Pioneers, 21 Activities (For Kids) by Pat McCarthy
Midnight on the Moon by Mary Pope Osborne
The Space Shuttle Program (Kid's Library of Space Exploration, Volume 9) by Kim Etingoff
Spaceships and Rockets: Relive Missions to Space (DK Readers Level 2) by DK
The Moon Book by Gail Gibbons
National Geographic Little Kids First Big Book of Space by Catherine D. Hughes
The Planets: The Definitive Visual Guide to Our Solar System by Robert Dinwiddie
Hello, World! Solar System by Jill McDonald
Planets by Ellen Hasbrouck
Astronomy for Kids: Planets, Stars and Constellations by Baby Professor
The Wondrous Workings of Planet Earth: Understanding Our World and Its Ecosystems by Rachel Ignotofsky
First Space Encyclopedia: A Reference Guide to Our Galaxy and Beyond by DK
Planets (Explore My World) by Becky Baines
National Geographic Animal Encyclopedia: 2,500 Animals with Photos, Maps, and More! by Lucy Spelman
The Animal Book: A Visual Encyclopedia of Life on Earth by David Burnie
National Geographic Little Kids First Big Book of Animals (National Geographic Little Kids First Big Books) by Catherine Hughes
Animals: A Visual Encyclopedia, Second Edition by DK

Ocean: A Visual Encyclopedia by DK
Everything You Need to Know about Dinosaurs by DK
Merriam-Webster's Elementary Dictionary by Merriam-Webster
Merriam-Webster Children's Dictionary: Features 3,000 Photographs and Illustrations by DK
Scholastic Children's Dictionary by Scholastic
Children's Illustrated Dictionary by DK
Scholastic Pocket Dictionary of Synonyms, Antonyms, Homonyms by Scholastic
First Children's Dictionary: A First Reference Book for Children by DK

CHAPTER 5

Pete's a Pizza by William Steig
The Little Red Hen (Makes a Pizza) by Philemon Sturges
The Princess and the Pizza by Mary Jane and Herm Auch
Just Grandma and Me (Little Critter) by Mercer Mayer
The View at the Zoo by Kathleen Long Bostrom and Guy Francis
If I Ran the Zoo by Dr. Seuss
If You Give a Pig a Pancake by Laura Joffe Numeroff
Lady Pancake and Sir French Toast by Josh Funk and Brendan Kearney
Pinkalicious by Victoria Kann
Grumpy Monkey by Suzanne Lang
Curious George by H. A. Rey
Gorilla Loves Vanilla by Chae Strathie
Arrow to the Sun: A Pueblo Indian Tale by Gerald McDermott
Sunshine Makes the Seasons (Let's Read and Find Out) by Dr. Franklyn M. Branley
Sun, Sun: The Joy of a Summer Day at the Beach by Brad Gray
Pete the Cat, I Love My White Shoes by James Dean
If You Give a Cat a Cupcake by Laura Joffe Numeroff
The Cat in the Hat by Dr. Seuss
The Day Jimmy's Boa Ate the Wash by Trinka Hakes Noble
Crictor by Tomi Ungerer
Mufaro's Beautiful Daughters by John Steptoe
The Three Little Pigs by Paul Galdone
Pigs by Robert Munsch
My Lucky Day by Keiko Kasza
Chester's Way by Kevin Henkes
Spider Sandwiches by Claire Freedman
Sam's Sandwich by David Pelham
Happy Birthday to You by Dr. Seuss

Happy Birthday to You, You Belong in a Zoo by Diane deGroat
Fancy Nancy: Puppy Party by Jane O'Connor
The Snowy Day by Ezra Jack Keats
The Magic of Friendship Snow by Andi Cann
The Mitten by Jan Brett
Chickens Aren't the Only Ones by Ruth Heller
Horton Hatches the Egg by Dr. Seuss
Green Eggs and Ham by Dr. Seuss
Rechenka's Eggs by Patricia Polacco
Goldilocks and the Three Bears by Jan Brett
Goldilocks and the Three Bears by James Marshall
The Magic Porridge Pot by Paul Galdone
Frog and Toad Are Friends by Arnold Lobel
Same, Same but Different by Jenny Sue Kostecki-Shaw
We Don't Eat Our Classmates by Ryan T. Higgins
Planting a Rainbow by Lois Ehlert
The Carrot Seed by Ruth Krause
Tops and Bottoms by Janet Stevens

CHAPTER 6

Kids' Paper Airplane Book by Ken Blackburn
Ultimate Paper Airplanes for Kids by Andrew Dewar

CHAPTER 7

Author: Eric Carle

- *Draw Me a Star*
- *The Mixed-Up Chameleon*
- *The Grouchy Ladybug*
- *A House for a Hermit Crab*

Author: Laura Joffe Numeroff

- *If You Give a Mouse a Cookie*
- *If You Give a Pig a Party*
- *If You Give a Cat a Cupcake*
- *If You Give a Moose a Muffin*

Author: Ezra Jack Keats

- *The Snowy Day*
- *Peter's Chair*
- *Pet Show!*
- *A Letter to Amy*

Author: Jonathan London

- *Froggy Gets Dressed*
- *Froggy's First Kiss*
- *Froggy Goes to the Doctor*
- *Froggy Plays Soccer*

Author: David Shannon

- *No, David!*
- *David Goes to School*
- *David Gets in Trouble*
- *It's Christmas, David!*

Author: E. B. White

- *Charlotte's Web*
- *Stuart Little*
- *The Trumpet of the Swan*

Author: Barbara Herkert

- *A Boy, a Mouse, and a Spider: The Story of E. B. White*

Author: Patricia Polacco

- *Thank You, Mr. Falker*
- *The Junkyard Wonders*
- *An A from Miss Keller*
- *The Art of Miss Chew*

Author: Kevin Henkes

- *Lily's Purple Plastic Purse*
- *Chrysanthemum*
- *Sheila Rae, the Brave*

- *Wemberly Worried*

Author: Jon Scieszka

- *The True Story of the Three Little Pigs*
- *The Stinky Cheese Man and Other Fairly Stupid Tales*
- *The Frog Prince, Continued*
- *Battle Bunny*

Author: Beverly Cleary

- *Ramona the Pest*
- *Ramona and Her Father*
- *The Mouse and the Motorcycle*
- *Runaway Ralph*

Author: Judy Blume

- *Tales of a Fourth Grade Nothing*
- *Superfudge*
- *Fudge-a-Mania*
- *Double Fudge*

Author: Gordon Korman

- *Ungifted*
- *Supergifted*
- *Swindle*
- *The Unteachables*

Author: Roald Dahl

- *Charlie and the Chocolate Factory*
- *James and the Giant Peach*
- *Matilda*
- *The BFG*

Author: Jerry Spinelli

- *Maniac Magee*
- *Wringer*
- *Loser*
- *Eggs*

Author: Jeff Kinney

- *Diary of a Wimpy Kid* (Book 1)
- *The Ugly Truth* (Diary of a Wimpy Kid, Book 5)
- *Cabin Fever* (Diary of a Wimpy Kid, Book 6)
- *Diary of a Wimpy Kid: The Getaway*

CHAPTER 8

Easy Reader Biographies: Betsy Ross: The Story of Our Flag by Pamela Chanko
Betsy Ross and the Flag (Landmark Books #26) by Jane (Rothschild) Mayer
A More Perfect Union: The Story of Our Constitution by Betsy Maestro
Our Government: The Three Branches (Social Studies Readers: Content and Literacy) by Shelly Buchanan
The Snowy Day by Ezra Jack Keats
A Chair for My Mother by Vera B. Williams
Rain (Seasons with Granddad) by Sam Usher
Hurricane by David Wiesner
Arrow to the Sun by Gerald McDermott
The Pueblo (True Books) by Kevin Cunningham
Totem Tale: A Tall Story from Alaska by Deb Vanasse
North American Totem Poles: Secrets and Symbols of North America by Molly Perham
One Day in the Tropical Rainforest by Jean Craighead George
A Walk in the Rainforest (Biomes of North America) by Rebecca L. Johnson
I Like Art: Renaissance by Margaux Stanitsas
I Like Art: Expressionism by Margaux Stanitsas
Spot the Differences Book 3: Art Masterpiece Mysteries by Dover (Dover Children's Activity Books)
Gregory the Terrible Eater by Mitchell Sharmat
Chocolate Fever by Robert Kimmel Smith
Rafi and Rosi Carnival! (Dive into Reading) by Lulu Delacre
Puerto Rico by Deborah Kent
A Cache of Jewels and Other Collective Nouns by Ruth Heller
A Compendium of Collective Nouns: From an Armory of Aardvarks to a Zeal of Zebras by Woop Studios
Planting a Rainbow by Lois Ehlert
The Kids' Guide to Exploring Nature (BBG Guides for a Greener Planet) by Brooklyn Botanic Garden Educators

Monarch Butterfly by Gail Gibbons
The Monarch: Saving Our Most-Loved Butterfly by Kylee Baumle
The Life Cycles of Butterflies: From Egg to Maturity, a Visual Guide to 23 Common Garden Butterflies by Judy Burris

CHAPTER 9

The Three Billy Goats Gruff by Paul Galdone
Caps for Sale by Esphyr Slobodkina
Millions of Cats by Wanda Gag
Hurricane Heroes in Texas by Mary Pope Osborne
Where the Wild Things Are by Maurice Sendak
Arrow to the Sun by Gerald McDermott
The Mouse and the Motorcycle by Beverly Cleary
Charlotte's Web by E. B. White
Mufaro's Beautiful Daughters: An African Tale by John Steptoe
How to Train Your Dragon: How to Be a Pirate by Cressida Cowell
Swindle by Gordon Korman
Founding Mothers by Cokie Roberts
The Illustrated World Encyclopedia of Insects by Martin Walters
Animal Defenses: How Animals Protect Themselves by Etta Kaner
How Do Insects Protect Themselves? (Insects Close-Up) by Megan Kopp

CHAPTER 12

Wonder by R. J. Palacio
We're All Wonders by R. J. Palacio
Llama, Llama, Red Pajama by Anna Dewdney
Ira Sleeps Over by Bernard Waber
Fancy Nancy Saturday Night Sleepover by Jane O'Connor
Mallory's Super Sleepover by Laura Friedman

About the Author

Jennifer Lee Quattrucci is an early childhood and elementary school educator who has twenty-three years of experience teaching at-risk, Title 1 children in the inner city of Providence, Rhode Island. She is highly committed to providing exceptional, high-quality, developmentally appropriate educational experiences for all.

Jennifer believes that in a world where children are rushed from place to place, often occupied by devices, educators need to create an environment where children are given time and allowed to focus, think, create, and learn.

Her experience, reflection, and commitment to professional development has taught her that children must be nurtured and loved first and that no academic subject, content matter, or trend can replace the human connection all children need to thrive.

As a national DonorsChoose ambassador, Jennifer connects teachers in high-need areas with donors who want to help.

She is forever inspired by her husband, Jim, who is also a teacher in the inner city of Providence; their children, William and Angelina; and all the wonderful and diverse children she has had the pleasure to nurture and teach. The podcast *Educate the Heart with Jennifer Lee Quattrucci* was created as a companion to this book on anchor.fm/jennifer-quattrucci and is currently available on eight broadcast channels.

In her free time, Jennifer is a fashion enthusiast and blogs about maintaining a creative, personal style on a budget. She is the creator, owner, and author of the lifestyle blog mommyteacherfashionista.com.

Jennifer believes in the power of positivity and kindness.

www.ingramcontent.com/pod-product-compliance
Lightning Source LLC
Chambersburg PA
CBHW022012300426
44117CB00005B/146